STITCH CAMP

STITCH CAMP

18 CRAFTY PROJECTS FOR KIDS & TWEENS

LEARN 6 ALL-TIME FAVORITE SKILLS

sew 🧵 knit 🧶 crochet
felt 🪡 embroider ✂ weave

nicole blum &
catherine newman

Storey Publishing

The mission of Storey Publishing is to serve our customers by
publishing practical information that encourages
personal independence in harmony with the environment.

EDITED BY Gwen Steege and Michal Lumsden
ART DIRECTION AND BOOK DESIGN BY Carolyn Eckert
TEXT PRODUCTION BY Erin Dawson
INDEXED BY Christine R. Lindemer, Boston Road Communications

COVER PHOTOGRAPHY BY Mars Vilaubi, front, back flap (outside bottom), back (top right, background right, bottom), spine, endpapers (mandala sampler); and © Margaret Lampert, front flaps, back flap (outside top & authors, inside all), back (top left & right middle), endpapers (all except mandala sampler)

INTERIOR PHOTOGRAPHY BY © Margaret Lampert
Additional photo credits appear on page 192.

PHOTO STYLING BY Nicole Blum and Catherine Newman
ILLUSTRATIONS PAGES 9 AND 19 BY Ilona Sherratt

STOREY PUBLISHING
210 MASS MoCA Way
North Adams, MA 01247
storey.com

Printed in China by R.R. Donnelley
10 9 8 7 6 5 4 3 2 1

Library of Congress Cataloging-in-Publication Data

Names: Blum, Nicole, 1969– author. | Newman, Catherine, 1968– author.
Title: Stitch camp / Nicole Blum and Catherine Newman.
Description: North Adams, MA : Storey Publishing, 2017. | Includes bibliographical references and index.
Identifiers: LCCN 2017021162 (print) | LCCN 2017024142 (ebook) | ISBN 9781612127514 (ebook) | ISBN 9781612127507 (paper with flaps and 2 sheets of punch-out gift tags : alk. paper)
Subjects: LCSH: Sewing. | Needlework. | Textile crafts.
Classification: LCC TT705 (ebook) | LCC TT705 .B59 2017 (print) | DDC 746.4—dc23
LC record available at https://lccn.loc.gov/2017021162

For Ava and Ben and Birdy and Harry

CONTENTS

4 KNIT 101

Introduction:
GET
READY!

Get ready to learn old-fashioned skills!
Get ready to make fresh, fun projects!

When we started writing this book, it was called *Fiber for Kids*. We quickly enough realized that it sounded more like a breakfast cereal than a book — and not in a good way — so we renamed it. But fiber is still what this book is about: yarn, string, thread, and fabric, and the different crafts you can do with them, including sewing, embroidery, felting, knitting, crocheting, and weaving.

These are all old-fashioned (and just plain *old*) skills, but the projects in this book are fresh, and that's our favorite kind of combination! You can make lots of super-cool stuff, but you'll get a chance to unplug and unwind, to use your own two hands, to make awesome, inexpensive gifts for your family and friends, and to do something deeply satisfying that needs no batteries, doesn't involve a trip to the mall, and frees up your mind to talk or think or listen to music as you're doing it.

These are productive activities instead of consumer ones, which means that you're making things rather than buying them and using them up, and (as our own kids are sick of hearing about) there's pretty much no better feeling in the world than that. Are you simply *knitting some shoelaces*? No. You're becoming a more capable, resourceful, and creative person. (*And* you're knitting some shoelaces.)

We're covering what we think of as the basics. Our idea is that you can pick up this book and learn any of the skills you need to make all of the projects in these pages, before going on to be lifelong sewers and weavers, knitters and crocheters. (What? Is that too much to ask?)

The chapters don't need to be followed in any particular order, but we've organized each chapter from the easiest project to the hardest, so that you can build skills as you go. If you want to skip around, that's fine; you might just have to refer back to an earlier instruction to learn the necessary skill. You may also need to refer to other chapters as you work, because many of the projects involve more than one type of craft. In other words, you will felt in the knitting chapter, sew in the crocheting chapter, and embroider in the felting chapter.

You'll see that we have lots of instructions in these pages, but we also want to encourage you to *improvise* (make something up) and experiment: to *not* follow the rules, to figure out a way that works better for you, to adapt and adjust so that everything is just how you want it to be. You will make mistakes along the way, and that's perfect — not only because that's how you learn and that's how you understand the problems that need solving, but also because that's how you invent new techniques and better ways of doing things.

We have lots of instructions in these pages, but we also want you to improvise and experiment: to *not* follow the rules, to figure out a way that works better for you.

GETTING STARTED

Because these six crafts require different materials and skills, we're introducing each one separately in the chapters that follow. But whichever craft you choose to do, you will need materials, and we can't help recommending that you be as thrifty and resourceful and recycle-y as possible!

LOOK UP!

If you're reading this book and you see a term you don't know, try looking it up in the glossary (page 186) or index (page 193).

BUSY HANDS = HAPPY BRAIN

Kelly Lambert is a scientist who studies the body's nervous system and has spent a lot of time researching the connection between doing stuff with your hands and feeling happy. Her conclusion is that when we perform activities that our brains think of as life-sustaining — providing shelter, making food, creating clothing — our bodies release chemicals in the nervous system called dopamine and serotonin, which make us feel good. (That's your brain rewarding you for taking care of important tasks.) Do sewing, knitting, and other fiber crafts count? Yup.

As she puts it, "Our brains have been hardwired for this type of meaningful action since our ancestors were dressed in pelts."

So craft with fiber because it's fun, because there's something you want to make — or just because it will make you feel good.

Gather materials from your home — think old sheets, odds and ends of string and yarn, outgrown clothes that can be cut up — and from generous relatives who have fabric stashes you can raid or knitting needles they're not using right now. Look in thrift shops and flea markets for craft supplies, fabrics, and T-shirts and sweaters that can be recycled into yarn and fabric, as well as more basic tools, such as needles and hooks.

We like recommending recycled materials because you're just learning and you might need to start over — and an old T-shirt is a less stressful thing to have sewn badly than a piece of new, expensive fabric.

But we have a slightly mixed message here (sorry) because, while we want you to use what you have or can adapt, we also want you to love the material you're using! These are *slooooow* crafts, which means that you'll be spending a lot of time with them. If you feel like your yarn is ugly or scratchy, that time's going to be less fun than if your yarn is super soft and your favorite color. Find the right balance for yourself of using what you have and investing in a few quality materials that you absolutely adore.

Our other main piece of advice for getting started, regardless of the craft you're doing, is to be patient: patient learning and patient doing. You know the expression, "It's the journey, not the destination"? That's what crafting is.

You're not knitting a hat simply to end up with a hat. If that were true, you could just buy one for a dollar from your local thrift store. You're knitting a hat because knitting is a deeply satisfying thing to do. (Very Zen, right?) Try to remind yourself of this if you find yourself rushing, wishing something would be done already, or on the verge of giving up. There's time; take it. So make sure you're comfortable! Warm enough or cool enough. In a work space that has plenty of light. Sitting in a way that doesn't tire your back. Working with a nice big glass of bubbly water or a mug of hot tea beside you and, maybe, a bowl of popcorn, because snacks are important.

WHAT? FIBER!

All kinds of things are made from fiber. Take a quick walk around your house and you'll see lots of examples: sheets, blankets, couches, chairs, drapes, clothing, bath mats, dishcloths, shower curtains, carpets — and all of it's been knit, woven, crocheted, or felted by someone (or, you know, by a *giant machine*). Touch these items and look closely, and you might be able to figure out where the fiber came from. Fiber can come from many sources, but these are the main ones:

ANIMALS. The fleece or hair of sheep, goats, alpacas, llamas, rabbits, and camels is spun to make wool, mohair, cashmere, alpaca, llama, and angora yarn and other materials, depending on the animal it comes from.

WORMS. Thread is unraveled from silkworm cocoons to make silk yarn or thread.

PLANTS. Material from the stalks and seedpods of cotton, hemp, jute, and flax is spun to make cotton, hemp, jute, and linen yarn, thread, or string.

HUMAN-MADE MATERIALS. Fine strands of glass, metal, and plastic are processed in a variety of ways to make fiberglass, steel wool, acrylic, polyester, nylon, synthetic fleece, and more.

TIP ‹ WHEN IN DOUBT

Many of our projects call for recycled materials that you'll cut up and stitch over. You probably know what's okay in your house, but ask a parent if you're not sure. (You don't want to cut something up only to find out it was your mother's favorite college T-shirt.)

SOLO OR SOCIAL

One thing we love about fiber crafts is that they're fun to do in a totally solitary, quietly thoughtful way *and* they're fun to do with a friend or even a group of friends. Informal craft parties and get-togethers are super delightful, and they can be especially great for learning new skills, asking questions, and getting help with the project you're working on.

We also recommend bringing your project with you wherever you go, partly because it's satisfying to pull out your knitting while you're waiting for the orthodontist (hello, time not wasted!), and partly because you may end up in the company of a person who knows a lot about it.

We have to confess: we love this book, and we've done our very best to make the instructions clear, but there is still no substitute for learning these skills from a real, live human. Your siblings, parents, grandparents, aunts and uncles, cousins, teachers, babysitters, counselors, and friends are the greatest resources you've got. Ask around to see who knows how to do what — and then ask that person to teach you! It's one of the best ways to learn, and it offers an amazing chance to deepen your relationships — especially with older people who are sick of asking for help with their smartphone and who will relish an opportunity to teach *you* something for a change.

You're not knitting a hat simply to end up with a hat. You're knitting a hat because knitting is a deeply satisfying thing to do. Try to remind yourself of this if you find yourself on the verge of giving up.

HELPFUL RESOURCES

Besides human teachers and this book you're holding, there are lots of other places to turn, should you need help learning or mastering a skill.

- **FIBER SHOPS.** Yarn and fabric shops often offer classes to crafters of all levels, and you could ask for one for your birthday or for a holiday gift. They're also staffed with helpful people who can guide you to the right supplies and, if they're not super busy, answer some of your basic questions or help solve a problem.

- **WEBSITES.** There are free and subscription-based websites of all kinds that can help you learn skills and think up ideas for projects.

- **YOUTUBE VIDEOS.** These are great for skills that are sometimes hard to learn from the page, especially when it comes to crocheting and knitting.

- **OTHER BOOKS.** On the off chance this book doesn't have every last thing you need in it (*what?!*), look through the shelves in your local library, in both the kid and adult crafts sections. We offer some suggestions in the Additional Reading section on page 188.

- **THIS BOOK!** That's kind of a joke, but actually, there's a glossary on page 186, so if you find a word you don't know, and we don't refer you somewhere else to explain what it is, it just might be there.

HEY, YOU LEFT-HANDED LOVIES!

If you are learning skills and following the steps and they feel wrong to you, then you might want to experiment with switching hands. (This is likely to be especially true in the Crochet chapter.) Every time the instructions says *left hand* think *right hand*, and vice versa. Likewise, when the instructions simply refer to *left* and *right*, try reversing them (you can even make notes right in the book, if that helps). If the visual how-tos become hard to follow, try looking at the illustrations in a mirror so that they'll correspond to the hands you're using.

KNOTTY BY NATURE

We didn't include a chapter on knots in this book because, while we think of knots as a *skill*, we don't really think of them as a *craft* — maybe because knots tend to be about solving problems, while crafts tend to be about making things. But some knots are used in crafting and some crafts are entirely based on knots: macramé, for example, and some friendship bracelets.

Suffice it to say, we love knots, and knowing a couple of them is vital if you're going to be sailing, camping, or mountain climbing (as well as, you know, doing the fiber crafts in this book). Besides, they're fun to learn.

SQUARE KNOT

A square knot is a strong and attractive way to tie together two ends of a string or rope. It's an important knot for sailors and scouts, and it's also used decoratively, for tying sashes and in macramé.

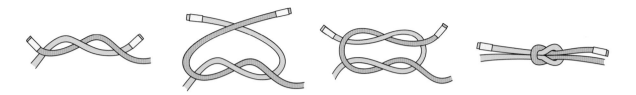

CLOVE HITCH

Used by boaters and climbers, this is a great knot for tying a rope to a pole (or a horse to a post).

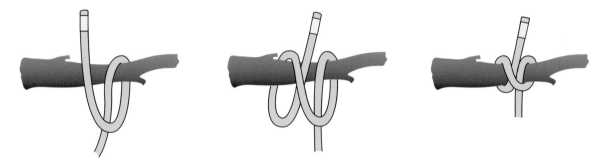

BOWLINE KNOT

This is a reliable way to make a loop at the end of a string or rope. It's especially useful because it's strong, but also really easy to untie when you're done with it. Sailors refer to it as the *King of Knots*.

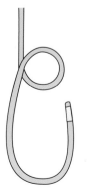

SEW

Look at the shirt or jeans you've got on: wherever there's a seam — two pieces of fabric attached together — that's sewing. If you look closely on the underside of the fabric, you probably can see the stitches holding the two pieces together.

Sewing comes first in this book because we think of it as a basic life skill, somewhere between breathing and, maybe, fixing a bike! Once you acquire some basic sewing know-how — like threading a needle, knotting your thread, and making a couple of simple stitches — you can do all kinds of useful things, such as mend your jeans, stitch a patch to your scout

uniform, or add a button to your favorite bag so it will stay closed. To say nothing of the *fun* things you'll be able to do! Like make your own clothing or Halloween costume, craft cute gifts for your friends and family, and, well, whatever you dream up.

We're also starting with sewing because you'll need basic sewing skills to finish or decorate many of the other projects in this book, even those that start with a different fiber craft, such as knitting or weaving. For example, you'll need basic sewing know-how to tackle the embroidery projects in chapter 2 and to sew up the felt projects in chapter 3! Luckily, this chapter will teach you what you need to know.

GETTING STARTED

What You Need

Fabric. We mostly call for fabrics that don't fray or unravel around the edges, such as cotton jersey (also known as T-shirt fabric), felt, or polar fleece, because they're easy to work with and you don't need to hem them! Woven fabrics, like the kind button-down shirts are made of, are harder for beginners to work with, because they don't stretch at all, and they tend to fray at the edges. If you have a couple of big old T-shirts and a wool sweater you can shrink in the wash (see Felt the Fabric, page 83), you'll have all the fabric you need for the projects in this chapter. If you're using new fabric, it's a good idea to wash and dry it before starting your project, so it won't shrink later and surprise you.

Needles. You'll need a sharp needle with an eye large enough for the thread: an *embroidery* or *chenille* needle is a good bet; don't use a *tapestry* needle, which has a rounded, rather than sharp, point. (Trying to sew with a dull needle is very frustrating.) A stray piece of felt is a good place to keep your needles, or (once you learn to sew) you can stitch a couple of rectangles of felt down the middle to make a "book" for storing them.

Thread. We like embroidery floss (also called embroidery thread) because it comes in a million colors, and because you can separate its six strands by carefully pulling them apart if you want to sew with something thinner. (See page 51 for tips on separating the strands.) Alternatively, we like Dual Duty Plus Button & Carpet thread, a very sturdy thread made by the company Coats & Clark.

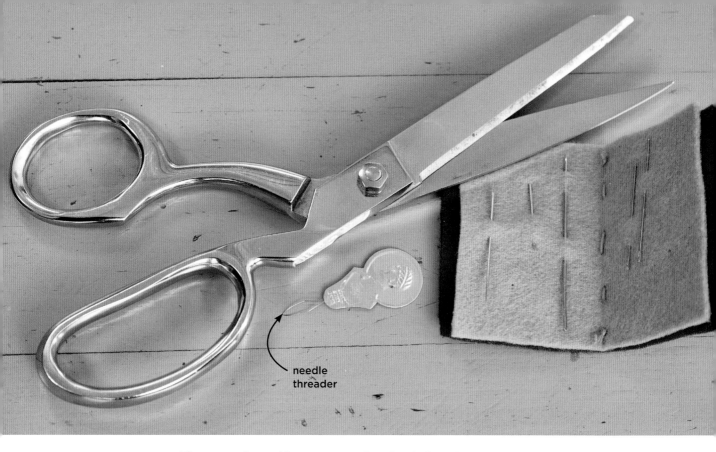

needle
threader

A needle threader. This optional item (shown above) is handy if threading needles is not your thing.

Scissors. Sharp ones are ideal; you'll need them for cutting both thread and fabric. (Cut paper with a different pair, since paper will dull them.)

White chalk or a disappearing-ink fabric marker. This will let you mark your fabric with the lines you want to cut or sew, while leaving you the option to change your mind or make a mistake.

Regular chalk can be sharpened with a large-mouthed handheld pencil sharpener so you can make finer lines, which you can simply brush off when you're done sewing.

A ruler or measuring tape.

Pins. Straight pins are useful for connecting a pattern to your fabric before cutting or for joining two pieces of fabric together before sewing. Keep your pins in a pincushion for easy access.

DID YOU KNOW? SEWING IS *OLD!*

In the Stone Age people in Europe and Asia sewed clothes from animal fur and skin, using needles made from antlers and bone, and thread made from other animal parts, such as sinew, which connects an animal's bones and muscles and probably made pretty strong thread. The sewing machine wasn't invented until the nineteenth century, which means that people were sewing by hand, and by hand only, for many thousands of years.

This bone sewing needle dates back to the second or third century.

THREAD YOUR NEEDLE

If you have a needle threader, great. But even if you don't, threading a needle is not difficult. For both methods, start by cutting an arm's length of thread; longer and it's likely to get tangled, shorter and you're going to run out quickly and be frustrated.

USING A NEEDLE THREADER

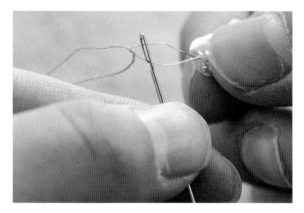

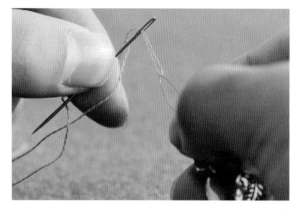

1. Push the pointy wire end of the threader through the eye of the needle. (The eye is the hole at one end.) Then slip your thread between the wires.

2. Pull the threader back out through the eye of the needle, making sure to hold one end of the thread to prevent it from working its way out of the needle. Pull the thread through so that you have a 6-inch tail.

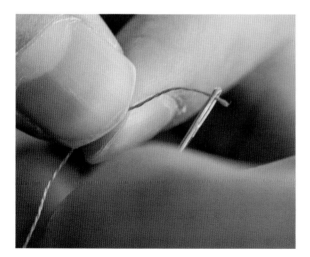

HAND THREADING

For hand threading, our preferred method is the old-fashioned "lick and thread." Gross as it might sound, when you lick the end of your thread, you get all the individual strands to stick together into a point, and it's easier to poke this into the eye of the needle. Lick one end of the thread, then push that end into the eye of the needle. Pull it through so that you have a 6-inch tail.

Regardless of which method you use . . . *voilà!* Your needle is now threaded. When you're pulling a stitch through your fabric as you sew, try pinching the eye of the needle to keep the thread from pulling out of it.

KNOT YOUR THREAD

This knot will keep the thread from pulling through your fabric when you start. The process works best when you begin by licking the end of your thread.

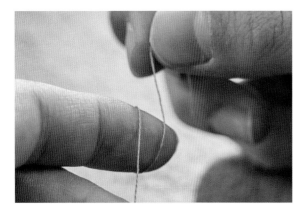

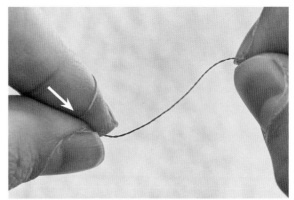

1. Use one hand to pick up the end of the longest thread tail. Wind the end of the thread around the pointer finger of your other hand.

   (To sew with a double length of thread, pull the short thread tail until it is even with the long tail. Then wind *both* ends around your pointer finger.)

2. Use your thumb to push this wound thread off your finger while rolling it slightly.

3. Pull the loop down to the bottom of the thread, where it should catch into a knot.

TIE OFF THE THREAD

When you get to the end of your sewing, you'll need to tie a knot on the underside of your project. Make sure to leave at least 6 inches of thread, or this will be very frustrating!

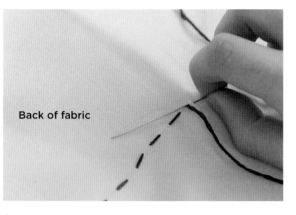

Back of fabric

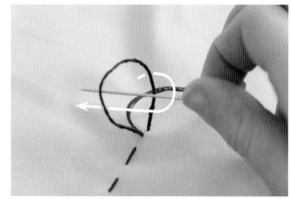

1. When you get to the end of your stitching (or near the end of your thread), turn your fabric over so you're looking at the back side. Make a tiny extra stitch so that the needle comes up through the place where your last stitch ended.

2. Before pulling the thread all the way through, poke the needle into the loop you just created.

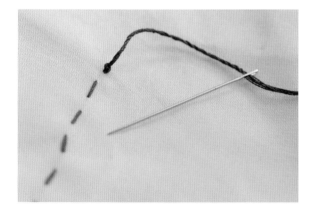

3. Pull the thread tight to secure the knot against the fabric and snip the thread close to the knot. Sometimes we repeat the knot before snipping, for extra security.

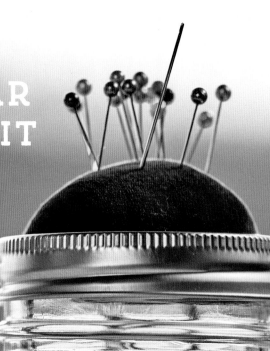

MASON JAR SEWING KIT

Make a sewing kit that
doubles as a pincushion!

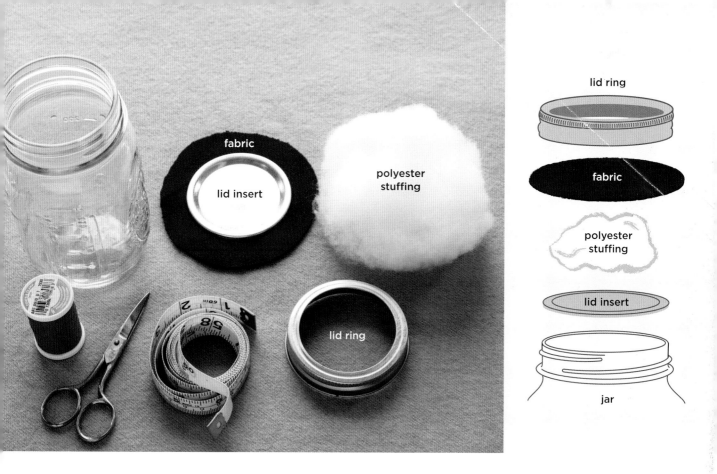

WHAT YOU NEED

- 1 mason jar (the kind with a two-piece lid)
- Fabric
- Hot-glue gun
- Polyester stuffing
- Sewing supplies to store in the jar

HOW YOU MAKE IT

1. Cut a fabric circle that's about 1 inch bigger all around than the lid of a mason jar.

2. Separate the lid insert from the ring, and wrap the fabric around the lid insert. Make a partial ring of hot glue around the bottom edge of the lid insert, leaving a few inches glue-less. Carefully press the fabric onto the glue to secure it.

3. Stuff polyester filling into the unglued opening until the fabric feels taut and cushiony, then finish gluing the fabric to the bottom.

4. Reattach the ring and screw it onto the jar. (Add a dab or two of hot glue to the underside of the ring if the pincushion seems inclined to fall out when you unscrew it.)

5. Now fill the jar with tiny scissors, thread, buttons, and safety pins — and stick your straight pins and needles in the top!

SEW A BACKSTITCH

The *backstitch* produces very sturdy seams that don't pull apart, making it a great stitch for securely closing up something like a beanbag (see page 21). It also produces lines of stitches so close together they look solid — perfect for tracing a drawing or writing. It's called a *backstitch* because with every stitch, your needle loops *back* to your previous stitch before making the next stitch forward. Try practicing on a scrap of fabric before stitching your project.

1. Thread your needle and knot your thread. Push your needle from the back of the fabric up to the front, pulling the knot tight against the fabric.

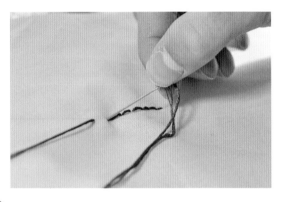 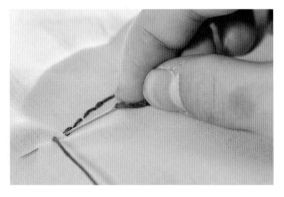

2. Push your needle down into the fabric ¼ inch behind where you started . . .

. . . and bring the needle back up through the fabric one stitch length ahead of your first stitch.

3. Repeat step 2 until you have the number of stitches you want.

TIP ⟨ TAKE A STRAND

One of the reasons we love working with embroidery floss is because it's so versatile. If you're filling in shapes or creating chunky designs, you may want to sew with all six strands of your floss, while other times — like if you're working a delicate design or a line of writing — you may want to work with only three or four strands of it. To make sure your stitches are secure, though, we don't recommend sewing with fewer than two strands. (See page 51 for how to separate strands.)

BEANBAG THAT IS ALSO A HAND WARMER

Toss them into a bucket and keep score — and they're toys! Heat them in the microwave and pop them in your pockets — and they're hand warmers! Either way, this is a fun project that comes together quickly, and it makes a great gift. Make your beanbag as big or small as you like, or vary the sizes for different projects.

WHAT YOU NEED

- Enough craft felt, polar fleece, or felted wool (see page 83) to cut a front and back piece
- Straight pins
- A small bowl (or a square cut from cardboard) for tracing (any size 3 to 5 inches is good)
- Chalk
- Scissors

- Embroidery floss or sturdy thread
- Sharp needle
- Rice or other grains, lentils or other small dried beans, or popcorn, for filling
- Kitchen funnel (optional), or a piece of paper or small spoon

FANCY IT UP

Embellish your beanbag with embroidery, if you want (see chapter 2). Just make sure to decorate your pieces of fabric *before* you sew them together and fill them up!

Instead of using your beanbag as a toy or hand warmer, you can add a tablespoon (about 12 grams) of dried lavender to your filling, call it a *sachet*, and use it to scent your dresser drawers.

HOW YOU MAKE IT

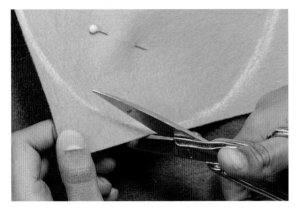

1. Stack or fold the fabric so there are two layers and stick a pin through the middle to hold the layers together while you're cutting. Trace the bowl or cardboard square onto the top layer with chalk. Keeping both pieces of fabric pinned together, carefully cut the shapes out. Taking your time here will make sewing easier, and you won't have to fix rough edges later.

2. Measure an arm's length of embroidery floss, thread your needle (see page 15), and knot the end (see page 16). Starting in between the two layers, push your needle up through the top piece of fabric and pull the thread through until the knot is snugly against the underside.

TIP

MATERIALS FOR HAND WARMERS

If you're planning to offer your beanbags up (or use them yourself) as hand warmers, use wool felt for the outside. Synthetics can behave strangely in the microwave, which is where you'll heat them up.

Rice is our favorite choice for filling hand warmers (it smells good when you heat it!), but whatever you choose, don't use popcorn! Guess what popcorn will do in the microwave. Go on. Guess.

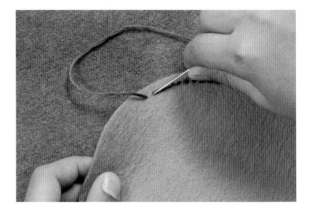

3. Stitch around the edge of both layers using a nice, even backstitch (see page 20). It is important to make your stitches very close together so the filling won't pop out, especially if you're using rice.

GUESS WHAT?

A really expert sewer helped us with this project, which is why it looks so perfect! Don't worry — our stitches never look as neat as this. And yours don't have to, either.

4. When you have about 1 inch left open, stop sewing but don't tie off your thread yet; just lay the needle and thread out of the way or push the needle into the fabric to keep it safe. Use the unstitched hole to fill the bag with rice, beans, or the filling of your choice. A kitchen funnel makes this easy, but you can roll up a piece of paper to make a funnel if you like, or just use a small spoon and some patience.

5. When the bag is full, finish stitching until you meet up with where you started, then tie off your thread (page 17) and snip it close the fabric. If it's important to you to conceal the knot, you can push the needle between the two layers before knotting.

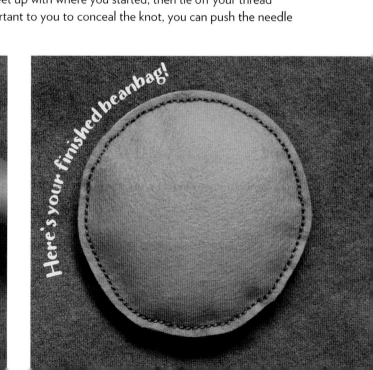

Here's your finished beanbag!

TRY THIS

Blanket stitch (see page 38) around your completed beanbag to add a neat decorative element. Or, if you prefer, sew the whole thing up with a blanket stitch or whipstitch (see page 25) instead of a backstitch — just keep your stitches nice and close together so the filling doesn't fall out!

backstitch + blanket stitch

whipstitch

TIP ▶ THE HEAT IS ON

To use your beanbag as a hand warmer, heat it in the microwave for one minute; if it's still not hot, try one more minute. *Be very careful when you remove it, just in case it gets hotter than you thought it was going to!*

SEW A WHIPSTITCH

A *whipstitch* is a quick way to sew together two pieces of fabric along the edge. It doesn't look as tidy as the blanket stitch, but it's easier. (Catherine uses it for *everything*!) Try practicing on a scrap of fabric before stitching your project.

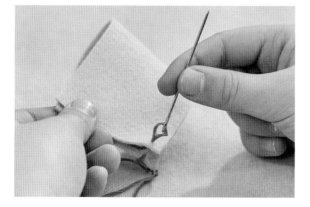

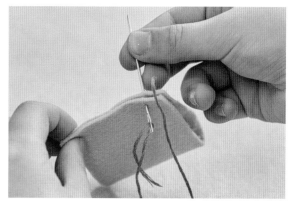

1. Thread your needle (see page 15) and knot your thread (see page 16). Then, while holding two pieces of fabric together, push your needle up from the back to the front of the top layer only, so the knotted end is tucked between the layers.

2. Now "whip" your needle around the edge of the fabric to the underside and push it back up through both layers, so that it comes up near your first stitch. You can sew from right to left or left to right — whatever is more comfortable for you.

3. Repeat step 2, doing your best to make even stitches that are about the same length and distance apart, as well as the same distance in from the edge of the fabric. (If they're not even, that's fine, too!)

TIP ▸ STITCH DISTANCE

Let the purpose of your sewing determine how far apart you make your whipstitches. If you're closing up something that has a filling or stuffing, you'll want your stitches to be quite close together so it doesn't spill out. But if you're using whipstitches to sew a fun patch onto your jeans, the distance between your stitches can be greater since they're more decorative than functional.

DIY Beanbag Toss

TO PLAY THIS FUN GAME,

you'll need three beanbags and three empty containers of varying sizes: a bucket, a flowerpot, and a soup can, for example. You can play by yourself, but it's more fun with other people.

SET UP

Use a stick (or tape) to mark a line on the ground (or floor). Then arrange the containers in a row starting about 10 feet away, smallest to biggest (about 6 inches apart), with the smallest closest to you, and the biggest farthest away.

PLAY

Take turns tossing all three of the beanbags and keeping score.

1 POINT
for the largest container

2 POINTS
for the medium

3 POINTS
for the smallest

The first person to get to 20 points wins.

FELT ENVELOPE

You can use a felt envelope for so many things: to store your jewelry, glasses, or Swiss Army knife; to wrap a small present or gift card; or as, yes, an envelope for giving (or keeping) an important letter. Feel free to use your own homemade felt (see page 83), just expect it to be a little less smooth and even than store-bought felt.

WHAT YOU NEED

- Straight pins
- Paper envelope, opened at the seams and unfolded
- Craft felt (You'll need a piece that's a little bigger than your unfolded envelope.)
- Disappearing-ink fabric marker or chalk
- Scissors
- Embroidery floss or sturdy thread
- Sharp needle

HOW YOU MAKE IT

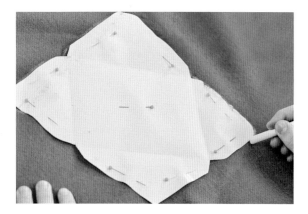

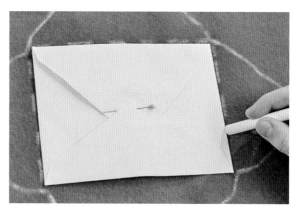

1. Pin the envelope along its edges to the felt, making sure to also put a pin in the center of the envelope, since you'll end up unpinning the edges. Use the marker or chalk to trace the outer edges of the envelope onto the fabric.

2. Unpin the edges of the paper envelope while keeping it pinned to the felt in the center. Then fold the envelope back up and re-pin the center. With a dotted line, trace around the outside of this rectangle. This line represents where you'll fold your finished felt envelope.

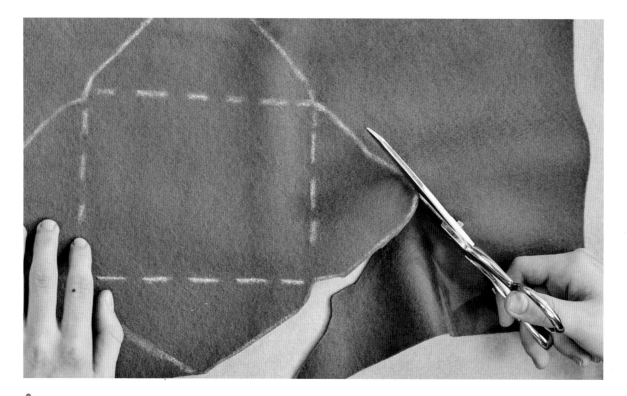

3. Remove the last pin holding the envelope to the felt and cut around the solid outside line.

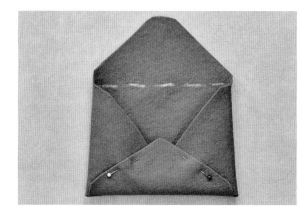 

4. Fold the cutout fabric on the dotted lines to re-create the envelope, then pin the envelope together as shown.

5. Measure an arm's length of embroidery floss or sturdy thread, thread your needle (see page 15), and knot the end (see page 16). Then push the needle up through one lower corner of the top layer of fabric, so that the knot ends up on the inside of the envelope.

Starting in that corner and taking care to not stitch all the way through the front of the envelope fabric, use a running stitch (see page 33) to sew the bottom flap up from one corner and down to the other corner.

6. Tie off the thread on the inside of the envelope (see page 17). This is easiest if you poke the corner inside out first! Then snip the thread.

TIP RUNNING OUT OF THREAD MIDPROJECT

As you sew, pay attention to how much working thread you have. Don't leave yourself less than 6 inches of thread to work with, or you'll be frustrated trying to knot it. But if you find yourself running out of thread before you're done with your project, don't worry. Simply tie off and trim your original thread on the underside of the fabric (see page 17), thread your needle anew, and start sewing again, pushing the needle up through the fabric near your last stitch.

Trying to use a really long piece of thread to avoid knotting off in the middle is a trick we've used — but it can backfire, since long thread tends to tangle and be really frustrating!

BUTTON UP

If you want your envelope to close securely, you can add a button.

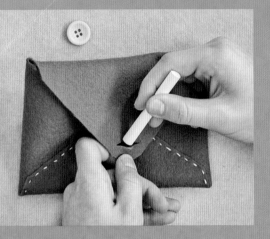

1. Near the point of the felt envelope's top flap, cut a very small slit for the button to go through. This slit should be smaller than you think you need. If you can't easily fit the button through, widen the slit very carefully and gently.

Fold the top flap down. Then with chalk, mark through the buttonhole onto the fabric underneath. That's the spot where the button will go.

2. Sew on the button (see page 34). Make sure to sew the button to the pocket only, and not to the front of the envelope.

3. Secure your buttonhole with the buttonhole stitch (see page 37).

4. Fold the top flap back over and push the button through the slit.

HOW TO
SEW A RUNNING STITCH

A *running stitch* is probably the most basic stitch there is! If you were going to draw something sewn, you might make a series of small dashes, right? Those dashes are running stitches. Try practicing on a scrap of fabric before stitching your project.

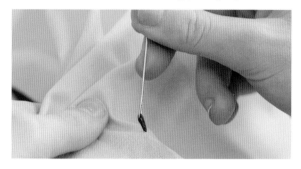

1. Push your threaded and knotted needle (see pages 15 and 16) up from the back of the fabric to the front, then pull until the knot is snug against the back of the fabric.

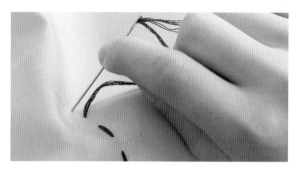

2. Push the needle back down into the front of the fabric.

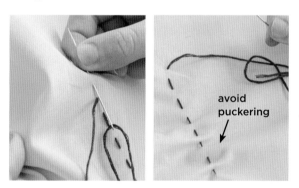

avoid puckering

3. Bring the needle back up through the fabric, about one stitch length from where it went in. To keep your fabric from puckering, be careful not to pull the thread too tight.

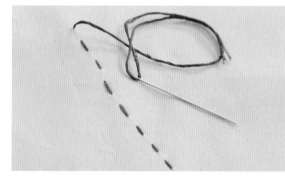

4. Repeat steps 2 and 3. That's the running stitch! Your sewing will look like a line of dashes with little blank spots between; turn it over, and it will look the same, since the same thing is happening on the other side.

TIP ◀ THE LONG AND SHORT OF IT

Where you push the needle in will determine how long your stitch is. Smaller stitches will join your fabric more securely, since there will be more of them, but longer stitches will take less time, since there will be fewer of them. For most of the projects in this book, we tend to think that ¼ inch is a good length for a running stitch: not too big, not too small.

HOW TO

SEW ON A BUTTON

There are two main types of button: a *shank* button has a little loop on the back to stitch through, and a *shankless* (or flat) button has two or four holes on its face that you stitch through. Both kinds are easy enough to sew on to fabric. *Keep your newfound knowledge to yourself, though, or you'll end up being your family's designated button-sewer-onner!*

SEWING ON A SHANK BUTTON

1. With fabric marker or chalk, mark where the button needs to go. Thread your needle (see page 15) and knot it (see page 16). Then push your needle up through the mark from the back of the fabric.

2. Bring the needle through the button's back loop and slide the button down the thread until the loop is up against the fabric.

3. Push the needle back through the fabric, very close to where it came up.

4. Bring your needle back up through the fabric, through the shank, and down into the fabric at least twice more to secure the button. Tie off the thread on the underside of the fabric (see page 17) and cut the thread.

SEWING ON A SHANKLESS OR FLAT BUTTON

1. Follow steps 1 and 2 for Sewing on a Shank Button, but instead of pushing the needle through the button's back loop, push it up through one of the button's holes.

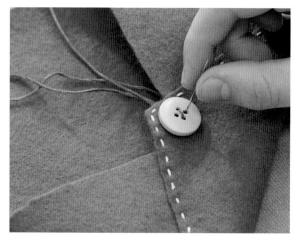

2. Slide the button down the thread until it is flat against the fabric, then push the needle down through another of the button's holes and through the fabric.

    Repeat steps 1 and 2 until you have sewn through all of the button's holes at least twice.

3. Tie off the thread on the underside of the fabric (see page 17) and cut the thread.

Here's what it looks like if the button has two holes.

SEW A BUTTONHOLE (OR BLANKET) STITCH

Since the slit you cut for the button might stretch out over time, it's good to reinforce it with a little bit of sewing. To do this, you will need to use the — wait for it — *buttonhole stitch*!

You'll use the exact same method to work *buttonhole stitch* and *blanket stitch*. The only difference is that you may want to space buttonhole stitches closer together than blanket stitches. Both are nice-looking options for joining two pieces of fabric along the edges when your sewing is going to show — or when you want to show off your sewing! Try practicing on a scrap of fabric before stitching your project.

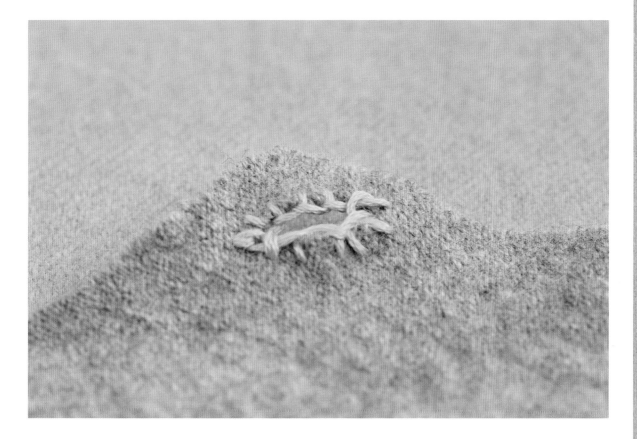

SEW A BUTTONHOLE (OR BLANKET) STITCH

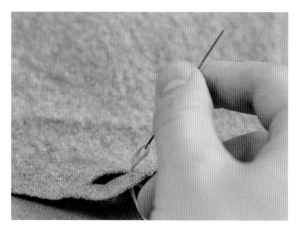

1. Thread your needle (see page 15) and knot the thread (see page 16). For a buttonhole, start at the right-hand side of the slit. Push the needle up from the back of the fabric and pull the thread through until the knot is snug against the fabric. For blanket stitch, you can hide the knot between the layers of fabric.

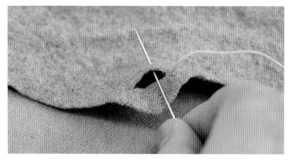

2. Bring the needle around the raw edge of the slit and push it up through the underside of the fabric about ¼ inch to the left of the first stitch, creating a loop.

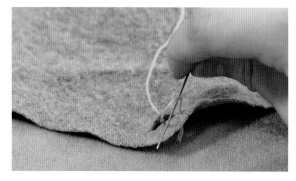

3. Pull the needle up through the loop, catching the thread so it stretches across the edge of the fabric, from one stitch to the next.

   The first stitch is always going to lean a little bit, instead of lining up like all the rest.

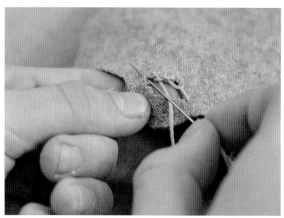

4. Repeat steps 2 and 3 to make even stitches. If you are working a buttonhole, stitch all the way around the hole, until you reach your first stitch. When you get to each corner of the buttonhole, push your needle up to make a stitch there, so you're not stretching the thread from one length of the buttonhole to the other.

   Tie off the thread (see page 17) on the underside of the fabric and snip the threads.

Hoo do you want to write to?

T-SHIRT ALCHEMY

Now that you know how to sew, you can recycle an old T-shirt into a cool oversize tank top, a sleeveless tunic, or (if you're game to add fabric to the bottom) a cute little dress. It just takes a snip here, a snip there, and a couple of lines of stitches. Start with a BIG shirt! We recommend raiding a parent's closet or making a trip to your local thrift store.

WHAT YOU NEED

- Extra-large cotton T-shirt, washed and dried
- A tank top that fits you well (to use as a pattern)
- Chalk
- Yardstick
- Sharp needle
- Embroidery floss
- Straight pins
- Scissors

Reverse Appliqué, page 45

Cross-stitch,
page 60

Appliqué, page 44

HOW YOU MAKE IT

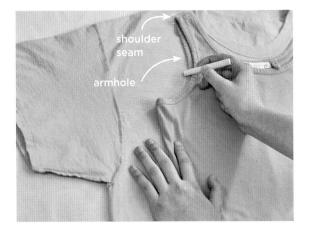

1. Turn the T-shirt inside out and smooth or press out any wrinkles. Lay the tank top on the T-shirt, up close to the neck of the T-shirt. With the chalk, trace around the tank's armholes and neckline and up over the shoulders.

2. Pull back the side of the tank top slightly, position the yardstick straight down from the armhole to the T-shirt's bottom edge, and draw a chalk line along it.

3. To create the tank top's flared shape, mark a point on the bottom edge 3 to 5 inches outside each marked chalk line. Use the yardstick and chalk to draw a new line connecting this point to each armhole. These will be the side seams of the tank.

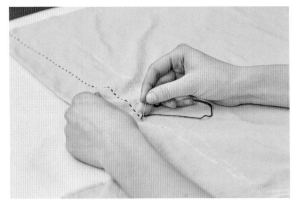

4. Thread the needle with embroidery floss (see page 15) and knot it (see page 16). Sew a running stitch (see page 33) on each chalked side seam and on each chalked shoulder seam.

   Secure the seams by starting and finishing your line of sewing with a few backstitches. Tie off the thread close to the fabric (see page 17), and trim the excess thread.

NOTE: If you want to be extra sure the T-shirt stays put while you're sewing, pin it along the side seam lines first.

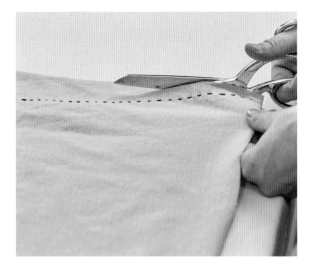

5. Taking care not to cut through any of your stitches, cut out the tank top shape, cutting about ½ inch from the sewn seams and on the chalked line of the armhole.

6. Turn your new tank top right side out, and you're done.

OR ELSE

To shorten the tank, simply measure, mark, and cut along the bottom edge before sewing. There's no need to sew a hem, because T-shirt fabric doesn't fray — and it rolls up a little bit in a way we love.

If you want to make a dress, lengthening is harder, but not impossible! Try sewing a wide band of fabric — cut from a different T-shirt — to the bottom edge of your creation.

Cut two bands longer than you need, then pin the wrong side of each strip to the right side of the shirt's bottom. With a yardstick and chalk, extend the flared shape of the T-shirt down along the bands. Sew the bands on with a running stitch about ½ inch from the original bottom edge before trimming the bands and stitching down where the sides of the bands overlap.

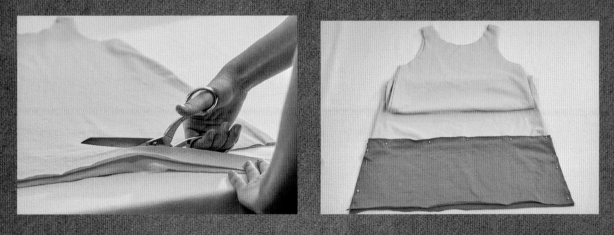

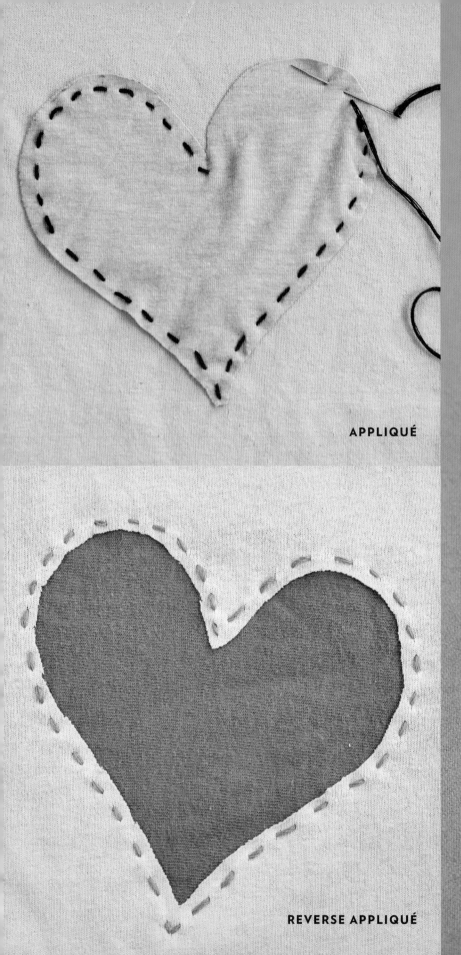

APPLIQUÉ

REVERSE APPLIQUÉ

FANCY IT UP

APPLIQUÉ is a fancy way to say *sewing on a fabric decoration*. It's a fun technique to add a little style and flair to your project. To get some more time with a favorite T-shirt you've outgrown, recycle it into a patch. Cut out the logo or name of your favorite summer ice cream spot, your team mascot, or the number from your sports hero's jersey — then stitch it on to something else.

There are two ways to do it: you can either sew a cut-out shape on top of your dress or tank (or bag or shirt or jeans) or sew a cut-out shape to the inside of the item you're going to wear — and then cut out the top layer to reveal a burst of contrasting color.

When stitching appliqué on top, we like to use running stitch (see page 33), whipstitch (see page 25), or blanket stitch (see page 38). You can also layer multiple sizes of the same shape, if you like, but it's easier if you first sew the varying sizes together before attaching them to your clothing.

Because **REVERSE APPLIQUÉ** is more involved, we thought you might like to see how it's done.

REVERSE APPLIQUÉ

There's blue
fabric behind
here!

1. With a fabric marker or chalk, draw or trace a simple shape, such as a heart or star or flower, onto your dress or tank (or bag or shirt).

2. From a different-color old T-shirt, cut a piece of fabric slightly larger than the shape you drew in step 1. Pin that piece behind your drawn shape, onto the underside of the front of your item. (The cut fabric will be sandwiched between the front and back of your item.)

    With embroidery floss, sew a running stitch (see page 33) around your drawn shape. Make sure you sew only through the top two layers of material, and *not* all the way through the back layer of your item.

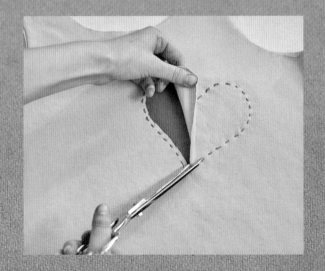

3. Pinch the front of the shape to separate the top layer from the one beneath, and snip into it with sharp scissors, then snip all the way around the shape about ¼ inch inside the stitched line, until the shape is cut free.

4. Remove the pins, turn the dress or tank top inside out, and trim off the excess fabric from the underside, leaving a ½-inch border. Turn it right side out, and you're done!

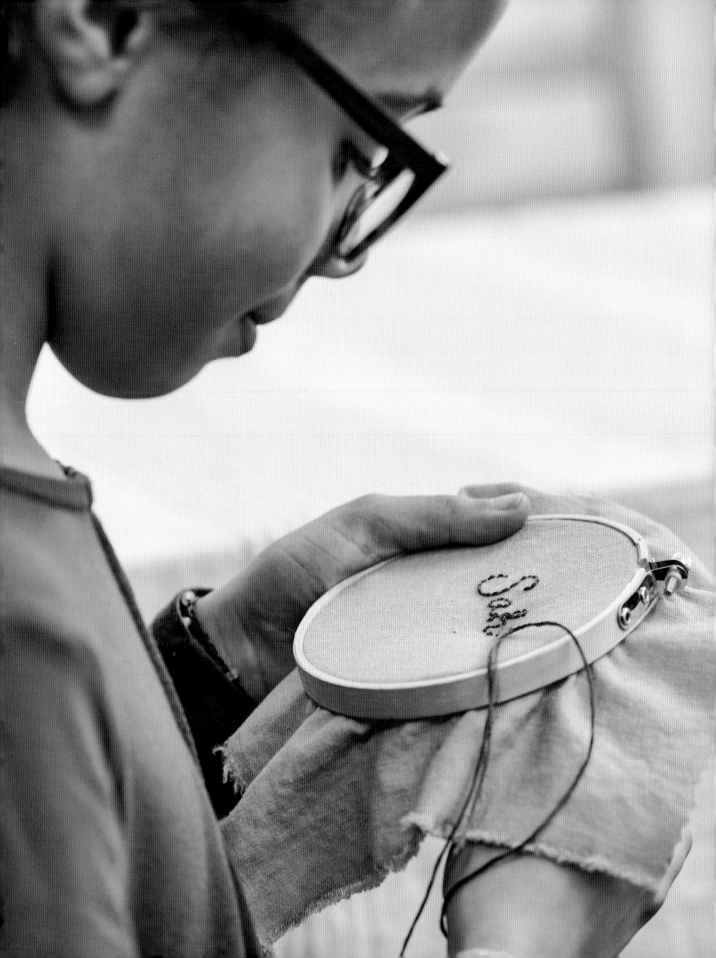

2

EMBROIDER

You can't *make* something with embroidery, but you sure can decorate with it! Got a plain shirt, dress, apron, dish towel, pillowcase, jacket, bag, or pair of jeans? Think of it as canvas for your stitched art. You've already learned a few basic stitches in chapter 1. Now we're going to teach you a few others so that you can draw and write with a needle and thread.

Embroidery is a great way to fancy up something made of fabric because it's easy, it's inexpensive, and it's a total expression of *you*: your favorite designs, your own drawings, a saying you love. And, if tomorrow (or next year) you don't like the result, you can pick out the stitches and start over.

DID YOU KNOW?

EMBROIDERY IS *OLD!*

Embroidered with silver, this silk cuff dates from the tenth century and was found in a Viking grave in Sweden.

Of course, soon after people learned to make clothes and mend them using basic sewing techniques, they figured out they could decorate them that way, too. Embroidery is an art that has been used around the world for centuries, with the earliest examples coming from China sometime between the fifth and third centuries BCE. An elaborately stitched piece of clothing from Sweden dates back to somewhere between 300 and 700 CE (that's more than 1,000 years ago). It includes running stitch, backstitch, stem stitch, buttonhole stitch, and whipstitch, though researchers aren't sure what, exactly, the stitches were used for: decoration or simply reinforcing the seams? Either way, those are all stitches we still use today!

GETTING STARTED

● ● ●

What You Need

Thread. Regular six-strand embroidery floss, or thread, comes in tons of colors and can be shiny and metallic or cottony and plain. (Sadly, the plain kind is the easiest to work with.) It's usually fairly inexpensive, so you can try a bunch of different kinds and colors. You can also use *perle cotton*, which also comes in lots of colors and thicknesses. It's often sold in *cones* or *tubes*, but sometimes comes in loose bundles called *hanks*. (To prevent the hank from becoming tangled, see Storing Your Embroidery Floss, page 51.)

Needle. You'll need a sharp *embroidery* or *chenille* needle with an eye large enough for the floss.

Needle threader. This is an optional, but handy, tool.

Scissors. Tiny sharp ones are great for cutting thread, but whatever scissors you have will get the job done.

Seam ripper. We aren't pessimistic at all, but this is a handy and inexpensive little tool for picking out your stitches if something happens to go wrong.

Embroidery hoop. This is an inexpensive adjustable wooden or plastic two-piece band used to frame the area you're working on, pulling the fabric taut so that it's easier to stitch. Embroidery hoops are readily available at fabric and craft shops and come in different sizes; a 5- or 6-inch hoop is a good, basic size to start with. (You can embroider without a hoop, though, and you might even prefer it! If you can, try it both ways.)

Disappearing-ink fabric marker, chalk, or pencil. Any of these will let you mark the lines of the drawing or writing you want to sew without ruining the fabric or showing through your final stitching.

Carbon transfer paper. This is for copying a complicated drawing or design onto your fabric before embroidering it, and you can get it at a fabric or craft store, where it is sometimes called *dressmaker's carbon*. Get darkly colored paper for transferring to light fabrics or white paper for transferring to dark fabrics. If you can't get access to carbon transfer paper, you can create a version of your own using just a pencil (see page 69).

Something to embroider! Because it won't stretch much while you're working on it, woven fabric is easier to embroider than knit fabric — think jeans, tote bags, and pillowcases rather than T-shirts and tank tops. Felt is also a good choice, as it's sturdy and doesn't fray.

HOW TO
USE AN
EMBROIDERY HOOP

An *embroidery hoop* is a two-part frame that stretches your fabric and holds it in place. You don't *need* to use one, but it might make your sewing easier. Try it and see.

To use the hoop, separate the two rings of the frame; this might require you to loosen the screw on the outer hoop. Lay your fabric across the smaller hoop, then press the adjustable hoop down over it, loosening the screw as necessary to let the hoops fit together. Pull the fabric taut, so that it is stretched tightly and smoothly. Then tighten the screw to hold the adjustable hoop in place.

If your design is bigger than your hoop, don't worry! You can just move your hoop, and eventually you'll get to everything in your design.

TIP: If you arrange your design so that the screw is at the top of the hoop while you're working, your floss will be less likely to catch on it.

smaller inside hoop   larger outside hoop   fit together

HOW TO
SEPARATE YOUR FLOSS

To separate the strands, cut the length of floss you want to use (we like an arm's length as a basic measure). Now separate the floss at the top into two equal sections of three strands each — or into two sections of two strands and four strands — and start to pull the sections apart gently and patiently.

The floss will spin as it unwinds, but to keep it from tangling, move your fingers down the sections as they separate until they are pulled apart completely.

TIP ▸ STORING YOUR EMBROIDERY FLOSS

Here's the truth: we both keep our embroidery floss in big resealable plastic bags, in colorful clumps and tangles — and that's okay! Part of starting a project simply involves untangling the color we want to use, unless we're lucky enough to find a fresh hank of it in the bag.

But there are many neater methods than ours. When you start a new hank of embroidery floss, try taking a few minutes to wind the whole length around something: a rolling pin, a rock, a clothespin, a card-stock gift tag, a wooden craft stick, or a piece of scrap cardboard with a notch cut into it to hold the thread end. You can still keep those in a big plastic bag, but they won't get tangled up in there.

MANDALA SAMPLER

If you were learning embroidery 100 years ago, you'd likely practice your stitches on a traditional sampler, the kind that has the whole alphabet written out in thread, with a flowery border. We love those! But our modern twist is less particular and more fun.

A mandala is a round design — *mandala* is the Sanskrit word for "circle" — that's a symbol of the universe. Pretty cool, right? You can use any stitches and colors to make up your pattern. Treat the hoop like a frame, if you like, and hang the whole thing on your wall. Or turn the mandala into a pillow, or stitch it to the back of your jean jacket or the front of a T-shirt.

WHAT YOU NEED

- Disappearing-ink fabric marker, chalk, or pencil
- Fabric to embroider that is at least a little bigger all around than your hoop. (Ideally this will be woven fabric with a nice open weave, such as burlap or linen, but a piece of an old bedsheet will work just fine.)
- Embroidery hoop
- Sharp needle
- Embroidery floss
- Scissors

HOW YOU MAKE IT

1. If you want to plan out your mandala, start by drawing your design onto the fabric with fabric marker, chalk, or pencil. Try tracing the inner ring of your embroidery hoop and then sketching out concentric (smaller and smaller) circles inside it. Or you can freehand the whole thing with your needle and thread if you prefer.

   Stretch the fabric across the smaller hoop (see page 50), then fit the adjustable hoop on top and tighten the screw.

2. Decide how many strands of floss to use. (See Separate Your Floss, page 51.) Then thread your needle (see page 15) with embroidery floss and knot the end (see page 16). Starting in the middle of your fabric, bring your needle up from the underside so your knot doesn't show.

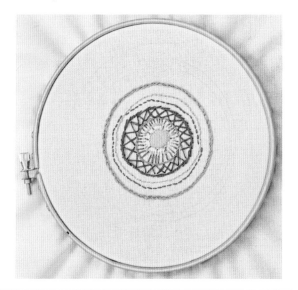

3. Create each circle with a different stitch pattern (see pages 56–63) or color. If you like repetition, you can also repeat the colors and stitches you like best — or make the whole mandala in one color.

   Whatever your design, begin and end your circles on the underside of the fabric, tying off and snipping the thread as you finish. When you are finished, remove the mandala from the hoop. (Or don't, so that you can hang it on the wall.)

TIP TWIST OF FATE

We learned this trick from a great sewer named Natalie Chanin: lick your thumb and pointer finger and run them down the length of your floss a couple of times before you knot, thread, and sew. This makes the floss less inclined to twist back up, which will make it less likely to tangle as you sew, which will make *you* a lot less frustrated!

HOW TO
SEW EMBROIDERY STITCHES

These are stitches you could use in any of our projects, not just the Mandala Sampler on page 54. You don't need to learn all of these stitches, just the ones you want to use. And there are many more embroidery stitches, too. If you have a friend or relative who knows embroidery, ask about the fern stitch, herringbone stitch, and bundle stitch — or look up other possibilities in a stitch dictionary or online!

Every stitch starts with the same first step: thread your needle (see page 15) and knot your thread (see page 16).

RUNNING STITCH	BLANKET STITCH	BACKSTITCH
See page 33.	See page 38.	See page 20.

SPLIT STITCH

This is a pretty stitch to use for outlining your designs. It's called the *split stitch* because your needle actually splits the floss as you sew. As with the backstitch, your stitches will do a little backtracking.

1. Push your needle from the back of the fabric up to the front, pulling the knot tight against the fabric.

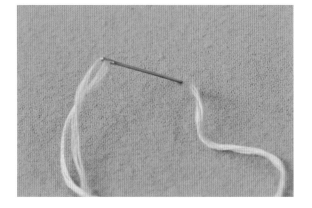

splitting previous stitch

2. Moving in the direction you want your line of stitches to go, push the needle back down into the fabric.

3. When you push your needle back up from the bottom, backtrack a little so that you push it through the stitch you just made, splitting the floss.

4. Repeat steps 2 and 3.

STEM STITCH

This is called the *stem stitch* because it's a classic choice for embroidering — that's right! — flower stems. It's similar to the split stitch (see page 56), only instead of pushing the needle back up through the stitch you just made, you will push it up just next to the stitch.

1. Push your needle from the back of the fabric up to the front, pulling the knot tight against the fabric.

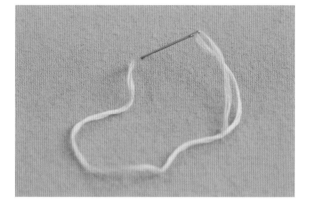

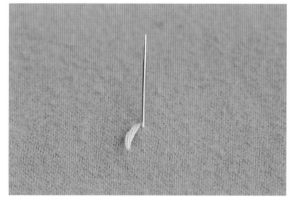

2. Push the needle back down into the fabric to make a stitch in the direction you want your line to go.

3. Bring your needle back up from below just slightly behind and to the side of the end of the stitch you just made.

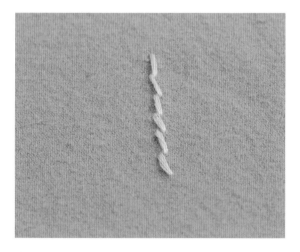

4. Repeat steps 2 and 3, always coming up on the same side of your previous stitch.

TIP

THICK AND THIN

The angle of each individual stitch will affect how thick or thin your whole line of stem stitching looks. For a thin-looking line, make your stitches straighter up and down. For a thicker-looking line, make your individual stitches slightly more horizontal.

SATIN STITCH

This is the stitch you use to fill in an area. Its close-together solid lines have a satiny look to them (hence the name). The shape you're filling in will determine the length of your stitches. For example, you'll fill in a leaf with very small stitches near the pointy ends and longer stitches at the wider middle. If you're filling in a large area, adjoining rows of shorter stitches often look nicer than a series of super-long stitches.

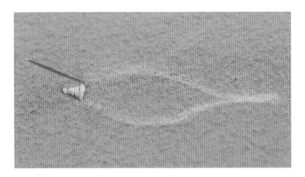

1. Draw an open shape, such as a leaf, onto your fabric. At one end of your design, push your needle from the back of the fabric up to the front, pulling the knot tight against the fabric.

2. Push the needle down into your line on the opposite side of the design from where you came up.

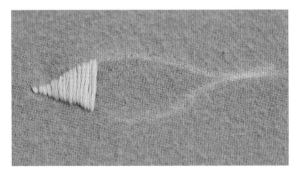

3. Bring the needle back up next to where you started the previous stitch, so that all your stitches are going the same direction (the back of the fabric will look more or less the same as it does on the front).

4. Repeat steps 2 and 3 until you have filled in your design.

FRENCH KNOT

This is basically like punctuation for your embroidery: the perfect period at the end of your sentence (literal punctuation!), sprinkle on your cupcake, dot on your *i*, eye for your whale, or little polka dot. It's one of those stitches that might slip away from you occasionally — you might think you get it and then suddenly realize you don't. Just keep practicing, and you will!

1. Push your needle from the back of the fabric up to the front, pulling the knot tight against the fabric.

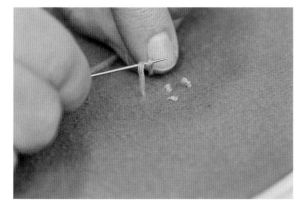

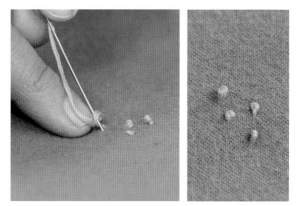

2. With one hand, hold the needle close to the fabric, and with the other hand, pinch the floss close to the fabric and wind it around your needle a couple of times in either direction: once will make a tiny dot, twice will make a bigger one, and three times is about as many as you want for a large dot.

3. Still holding the floss tight, push the needle back down into the fabric near where you brought it up. Keep pulling the floss tight so that as you pull the needle through the fabric, the wound floss slides off and makes a little knot against the fabric.

SEED STITCH

This is another way to fill in an area in your pattern, and it gives the space an interesting texture. It will look like you filled it in with a sprinkle of seeds! If you keep the stitches more or less the same length, that similarity will anchor the randomness of the stitch direction and placement.

1. Draw an open design such as a star or a cloud onto your fabric. Push your needle from the back of the fabric up to the front, pulling the knot tight against the fabric.

2. Fill in the shape with lots of short straight stitches, placed however you like, as close together or far apart as you want.

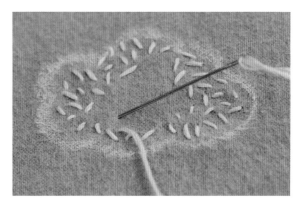

CROSS-STITCH

Some people embroider entire patterns with only little rows and clusters of cross-shaped stitches. This is called . . . *cross-stitching*! This fun little X-shaped stitch is a great one to use to decorate or accent your embroidery.

Making One (or Just a Few)

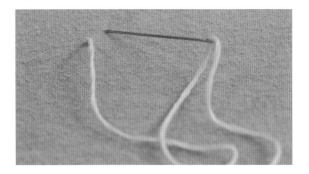 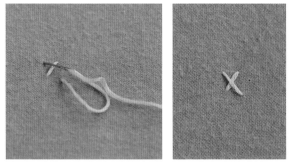

1. In the lower left-hand corner of where you want your X, push your needle from the back of the fabric up to the front, pulling the knot tight against the fabric. Push your needle down into the fabric where you want the upper right-hand corner of your X.

2. Come back up through to the front of the fabric in the lower right-hand corner of your X, then push your needle down again in the upper left-hand corner to complete the X.

Making a Whole Row

1. Draw two parallel lines on the fabric, about ¼-inch apart.

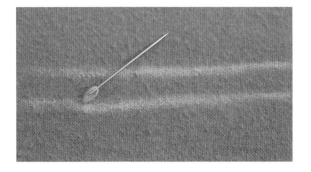 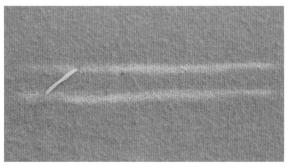

2. Push your needle up through the fabric to the front along the bottom line.

3. Push your needle back down into the fabric along the top line, to the right of where the needle came up. (How far to the right you stitch will determine the width of your crosses.)

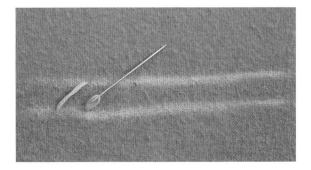

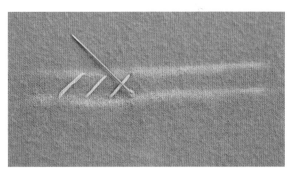

4. Push your needle up through the fabric directly below where you brought the needle into the fabric in step 3.

5. Repeat steps 3 and 4 until you have a series of diagonal lines.

6. You will now work in the opposite direction to complete the X of each existing stitch. Push your needle up through the fabric along the bottom line directly below where your last stitch ended.

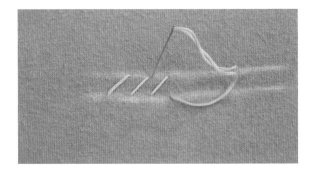

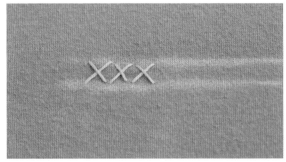

7. Bring your needle back down into the fabric along the top line, to the left of where your needle came up.

8. Repeat steps 6 and 7 to complete the row of Xs.

STAR VARIATION

Turn your X into a cute little star by making a third stitch, longer than your first two. Stitch vertically down across the point where the first two lines intersect. You can even add a fourth horizontal stitch, if you like, for an eight-pointed star.

CHAIN STITCH

A *chain stitch* makes a row of linked stitches that looks like a little chain. It's pretty as a decorative border or as a fancy outline. Most stitches move horizontally, but this one progresses vertically, top to bottom.

1. Push your needle from the back of the fabric up to the front, pulling the knot tight against the fabric.

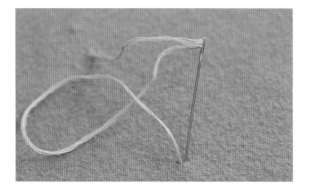

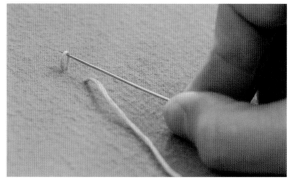

2. Push your needle down into the fabric as close as possible to the point where you just brought it up, without going through the same hole.

3. Before you pull the stitch tight against the fabric, push the needle back up through the fabric about ¼ inch below where you started in step 1. Push the needle through the loose loop.

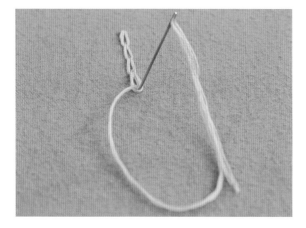

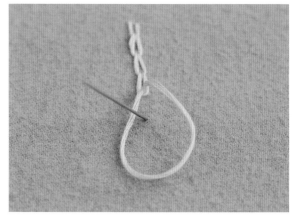

4. Pull the stitch snug, then push the needle down into the fabric inside the loop you just made, pulling the thread to create a new loop.

5. Push the needle back up through the fabric and loop. Repeat steps 4 and 5 as many times as needed.

DAISY STITCH

The technique for making *daisy stitch* is similar to that of a chain stitch (see page 62), but each link of the chain is separate from the others, and we think of them more as petals than links. Depending on how many loops you make and how you arrange them, you'll end up with a little flower or a butterfly.

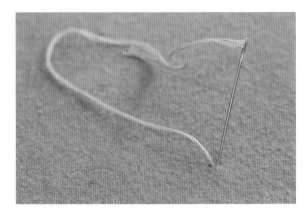

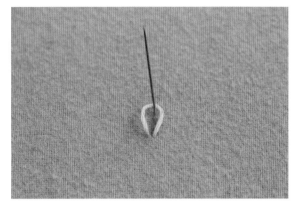

1. Push your needle from the back of the fabric up to the front, pulling the knot tight against the fabric. Push your needle down into the fabric as close as possible to the point where you just brought it up, without going through the same hole.

2. Before you pull the stitch tight against the fabric, bring the needle back up through the fabric about ¼-inch from where you started in step 1 and up through the loose loop.

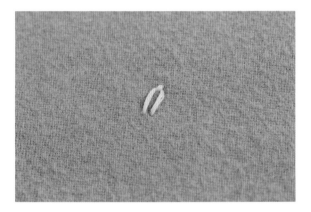

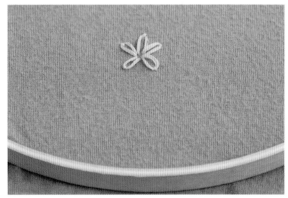

3. To secure the end of this single chain stitch, push the needle back down into the fabric on the outside of the loop of thread.

4. To start another petal, push the needle up to the front of the fabric near where you started your stitch in step 1. Repeat steps 1–3 as many times as you like (or can fit) for a flower. Or just make four loops to create a butterfly.

ART PILLOW

This project teaches you how to transfer a favorite drawing to a piece of fabric and then copy it with floss. We like to embroider a pillowcase, because then we get to see our handiwork every night (and morning)! But you can also embroider a dish towel — which makes a great gift for someone — an old-fashioned hanky, or even a button-down shirt.

WHAT YOU NEED

- A favorite drawing with simple lines or cursive writing (a very detailed drawing will be difficult to stitch, and large blocks of color will be difficult to fill in)
- Pillowcase (or handkerchief, dish towel, etc.), washed, dried, and ironed or smoothed flat
- Carbon transfer paper (purchased or homemade, see page 69)

- Tape
- Embroidery hoop (optional)
- Scissors
- Embroidery floss
- Sharp needle

HOW YOU MAKE IT

1. Transfer your drawing and/or cursive writing to your fabric using one of the methods described on page 69.

   Next, if you're using an embroidery hoop, stretch the fabric across the smaller hoop (see page 50), leaving a few inches all around. Then fit the adjustable hoop on top and tighten the screw.

TIP

SLEEPING BEAUTY

If you're making a pillowcase for the pillow you sleep on (or that someone else sleeps on), you can try keeping your embroidery along the edge of the open side, so that your face won't be directly on top of the bumpy stitches. (Or you can just turn the pillow over for sleeping!)

2. If there are parts of your design that need filling in, do that first. (If you don't plan to fill in your design, skip to step 3.) Cut an arm's length of embroidery floss. Thread your needle (see page 15) and knot the end (see page 16). Push the needle up from the back of the fabric to the front, and use satin stitch (see page 58) to fill in the design.

3. Stitch the shape outlines and writing. Cut an arm's length of embroidery floss and separate it into two three-thread strands (see Separate Your Floss, page 51). Thread your needle with one of the three-strand lengths (see page 15) and knot the end (see page 16).

   Push the needle up from the back of the fabric to the front and use the backstitch (see page 20) to follow the lines of your drawing (or the outline, if you filled it in with satin stitch first and want to emphasize the shape).

   For some designs, you'll likely need to tie your floss off on the back of the fabric at various points and go back to pick up parts of the drawing you missed. You can also hop from one place to the other on the back of the fabric, being careful not to pull your thread too tight.

   As you finish stitching your design, be sure to tie off your floss on the back and snip it.

WRITE WITH THREAD

Are you wondering why they bothered teaching you cursive in school? It's to make embroidering easier! Okay, that's not why, but it really does help with embroidery.

To embroider printed words, you have to stop and start between each letter, but to embroider words in cursive, you can follow them with your backstitch (see page 20) exactly the same way you wrote them. Handy, right?

For nice, clear writing, keep your thread thin (try sewing with three or four strands) and your stitches small, especially when you're going around curves. And don't worry if you were spared cursive in school — just try to connect your letters in a graceful way.

TIP ◄ CRISP BACKSTITCH

When using embroidery floss, we find that backstitched lines come out most sharply if you stitch with only three or four strands, rather than all six. (See Separate Your Floss, page 51).

TRANSFER YOUR DRAWING

You've got the perfect drawing for your embroidery project! Only how do you get it onto the fabric? There are two ways. Both options work best if you start by taping your fabric to a table, pulling it slightly to make the surface tight.

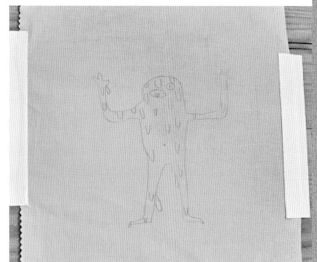

USE CARBON TRANSFER PAPER, which is sold at fabric shops. It has a layer of carbon (which kind of looks like pencil dust, but it might be blue, white, or black) on one side. With the drawing side on top and the carbon side touching the fabric, lay the carbon paper between your drawing and the fabric and pin all three layers together. Then trace the lines of your drawing with a dull pencil or, if you don't want to add extra marks to your drawing, a knitting needle.

The pressure of your pencil or needle will transfer carbon lines onto your fabric, which you can then embroider. (The carbon will likely rub off as you work. If your lines start disappearing before you're ready, go back over them with pencil.)

YOU CAN ALSO MAKE A VERSION OF CARBON PAPER YOURSELF. Use a regular graphite pencil to color over the entire back side of the page your drawing is on. (Use a photocopy of the drawing if you don't want to get pencil all over the original.) With your original drawing facing up, tape it to the fabric.

Trace the lines of the drawing with a dull pencil, pressing down firmly. Wherever you press, the graphite on the back of the drawing will transfer onto the fabric. Don't worry! Those marks will wash out of the fabric.

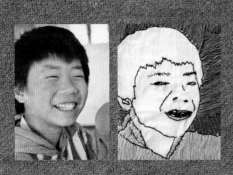

STITCHED SELFIE

Turn your old-fashioned craft toward a newfangled purpose with a little stitched self-portrait. To embroider a picture of yourself, follow the directions for the Art Pillow (see page 65), but start by transferring a drawing or photograph of yourself.

If you have a line drawing that you already like, you're ready to go — just resize it on a copy machine, if you want to. Otherwise, you can start with a photograph and use an image-editing program like Photoshop or a website or app to turn it into a line drawing that you can print and then transfer to your fabric. (At the time of this writing, there were several free options online for this. Try searching online for *picture stencil maker* to see what's available.)

Add to the design!

FABRIC HACK

If you have fabric, sheets, or clothing printed with flowers, a woodland scene, dots, geometric shapes, or anything else, you can use the pattern to practice your embroidery. Or you can use your embroidery to fancy up the pattern! Start by securing the fabric in your embroidery hoop (see page 50) if you like. Then try any one, or all, of these approaches:

TRACE THE DESIGN. Use embroidery floss and whatever stitch you like to trace around the shapes or to run up and down the lines of a plaid shirt. You can then fill your shapes in or not.

ADD TO THE DESIGN. Maybe your plain ocean waves need a couple of dolphins or a manta ray! Maybe those flowers need some ladybugs and those polka dots need some faces. Experiment with your stitches and colors.

CORRUPT THE DESIGN. Maybe you can't help stitching a wolf behind the window of the tea party or a UFO in the night sky — or turning a bird into a lovable witch. Do it!

SCOUT BADGE

You're good at lots of things: Settlers of Catan, writing, cats (like, being nice to them)! Whatever your skills and passions are, celebrate them with an embroidered merit badge. It's as easy as drawing something simple and coloring it in with thread.

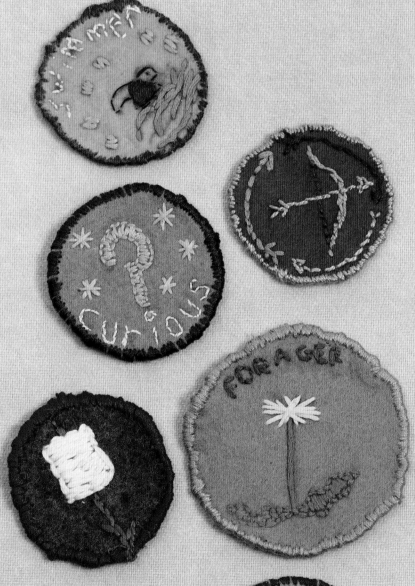

WHAT YOU NEED

- Circular object (like a mug or glass) for tracing (We like 2- or 3-inch circles for this, but you could make tiny badges or big ones!)
- Craft felt
- Chalk, disappearing-ink fabric marker, or pencil
- Small embroidery hoop (if you like to use one and your piece of felt is big enough)
- Sharp needle
- Embroidery floss
- Scissors
- Straight pins

HOW YOU MAKE IT

1. Mark a circle on the felt by tracing around the rim of a mug or glass. Then draw your (simple) design inside the circle using the chalk, marker, or pencil. If your design includes any written words, add those now, too. (You can also freehand the whole design by not planning or drawing it out before you start, but we're planners.)

   When you're happy with your design, stretch the fabric in the embroidery hoop (if you're using one) and tighten it (see page 50).

2. Thread the needle (see page 15) with an arm's length of floss and knot the end (see page 16). Push the needle up from the back of the fabric, and use any of the stitches on pages 56–63 to fill in your design.

   When you want to switch colors, tie off your floss on the back side of the fabric (see page 17) and cut it.

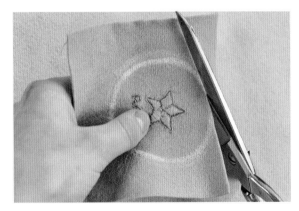

3. When your design is complete, remove the fabric from the hoop (if you're using it) and cut along the circle you made in step 1.

   GUESS WHAT? A really expert sewer helped us with this project, which is why it looks so perfect! Don't worry — our stitches never look as neat as this. And yours don't have to, either.

4. Rethread your needle with embroidery floss and whipstitch (see page 25) or blanket stitch (see page 38) around the edge of the circle. Or, if you want to attach your patch to a jacket, jeans, or bag, you can pin your finished badge to the surface you want it on and secure it all the way around using whipstitch or blanket stitch.

TIP

FILLING IN YOUR PATTERN

Your embroidered designs will come out sharpest if you fill in your pattern first (using, say, satin stitch, page 58) and then add outlines afterward using different stitches — like the backstitch (see page 20) or the stem stitch (see page 57). You can also add any details you like, such as daisies (see page 63) and French knots (see page 59).

FOR FUN

FLASHY MENDING

We love to mend things: we darn our socks and patch the elbows of our sweaters, the knees of our jeans, and even — sometimes — our furniture! This is partly because we're thrifty and partly because we don't like to waste old things that might just need a little extra love. It is very satisfying to fix something and keep using it.

But one other reason we mend things might surprise you: we love how it looks! Colorful patches and elaborate embroidery stitches make a piece of clothing fun and unique, and let you see the history in it — especially if you end up with layers and layers of decorative repairs. So the next time you end up with a hole in your jacket or a tear in your pants? Fix it, in as subtle or flashy a way as you like.

3

FELT

You've probably been using felt since you first picked up a pair of little-kid scissors, so you at least *kind of* know what it is. Felt is different from knit or woven fabrics because you cannot see the individual fibers that went into making it.

In fiber crafts, *felt* can mean a few different things. As a noun, there's *craft felt* — the thin, colorful fabric you cut into shapes or stick on a felt board to make a story — which is usually made out of acrylic. At fancier shops and online you can get *wool craft felt*. Wool felt is very

nice to work with — sturdier, smoother, and often in better colors than acrylic felt — and it's perfect if you're making something that you want to use and keep for a long time. (It's also more expensive than acrylic.)

This chapter is about *felt you make yourself* from fabrics or garments that have been knit, crocheted, or spun with animal fibers. This gets us into using *felt* as a verb. When washed in hot water, many animal fibers — including wool, cashmere, and alpaca — tangle together and turn into a dense mat-like fabric. You can do this with pure fleece straight from a sheep or with existing fabric or garments. Felted fabric is warm, won't fray when you cut it, and is super easy to sew! (A favorite sweater that you accidentally shrank in the wash will be perfect to use for the projects in this chapter.)

DID YOU KNOW? FELTING IS *OLD*!

Archaeologists at a site in Turkey can date the ancient felt they've found to 6500 BCE (more than 8,000 years ago). More fun, though, are the legends that *claim* to explain felt's origins:

- When Saint Clement and Saint Christopher fled persecution in the first century CE, they packed their sandals with wool fleece to prevent blisters. Upon arrival at their destination, they discovered that the movement and sweat had turned the wool into felt socks!

- While stuck on Noah's Ark, the sheep, goats, and other animals shed their fleece and trampled it with their hooves. Later, Noah found the entire floor carpeted in felt!

GETTING STARTED

What You Need

Sweaters made entirely of wool, cashmere, alpaca, and/or angora. Don't worry — on page 83, we'll tell you how to find these.

Access to a washing machine and dryer. This is how you'll felt the sweaters (see page 83). You can definitely take your sweaters to a laundromat, but bring extra quarters (and a good book) in case they don't felt on the first try.

Sewing supplies (see page 13), including a sharp needle and embroidery floss, scissors, chalk, and straight pins. All of the projects in this chapter start with felting but end with sewing.

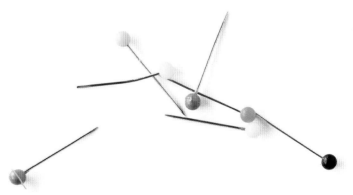

HOW TO
GET THE SWEATERS

Dig through your closets, hit up friends and relatives, and go to thrift shops to find sweaters made of 100 percent wool, alpaca, cashmere, and/or angora. Some labels specify the kind of wool the sweater is made of. Lamb's wool is our absolute favorite. Merino wool is also excellent. Shetland wool is finicky but will, with persistence, felt. Super-soft cashmere is lovely when it works but is also a bit tricky since it can resist felting. Angora is a kind of yarn made from rabbit fur, and while you're unlikely to find a sweater made only with angora, it's great if there's some mixed into your wool because it will felt beautifully and be *very* fuzzy.

Don't use sweaters made of other natural fibers (such as cotton or linen), or from synthetic fibers (such as acrylic or nylon) — even if only used in small percentages — because they will be more likely not to felt at all or to *pill*, which means get covered in small, hard lumps.

The bigger the better, because once the sweater shrinks, it will get very small. And skip anything labeled *washable*, because that means it's most likely been treated with chemicals that prevent shrinking and felting. Don't worry about small holes, which will disappear, or rips or stains, which can be cut away after felting. Cardigans are fine to use, and it can be fun to keep the buttons in your projects!

HOW TO
FELT THE FABRIC

When you wash and dry it, feltable fabric will shrink, lose its stretchiness, and get nice and tight, with all the fibers matted together so that you can cut the fabric and it won't stretch or fray. However, this doesn't always happen the first time you wash and dry wool, so be patient. Some sweaters require multiple trips through the washer and dryer. Here's how:

WASH THEM. Put the sweaters in the washing machine with enough laundry detergent for a normal load. We sometimes also put in a pair or two of jeans for added abrasiveness, which increases fiber-matting tendencies.

Do a hot wash with a cold rinse — the temperature swing helps the fibers seize up and stick together. And if you have any other setting choices to make, choose the most vigorous ones, with as much agitation and spinning as possible. If your parents are worried about getting a lot of wool lint in the machine, you can put the sweaters in a pillowcase before you wash them.

DRY THEM. Put the sweaters in the dryer and dry them on high heat.

EVALUATE THEM. If they are still stretchy or if you can still see the individual knit stitches in the sweater bodies, then they're not felted. Back into the washer! Keep at it. Some will give in eventually, and others won't. For certain hard-to-felt specimens, we have even boiled sweaters in a big pot of water — which makes the house smell like a sheep in a thunderstorm, so we don't recommend it.

If you have sweaters that don't seem thick and felted after repeated attempts, *do not use them for the projects in this chapter* — no matter how gorgeous they may be. We speak from experience here: a sweater that is fraying or stretching will be so frustrating to sew with that you will rue the day you decided to use it anyway.

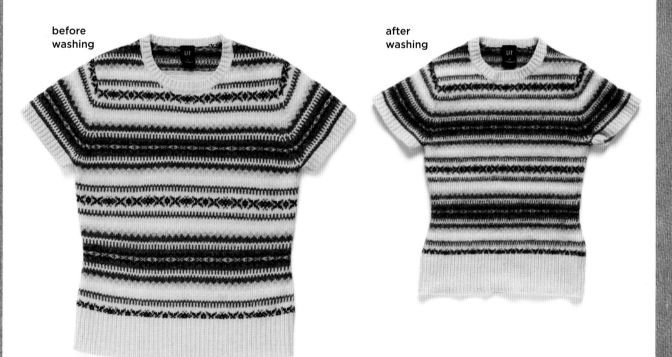

before washing

after washing

THE DRYER LINT CHALLENGE

Okay, this is not a project, it's a question: *what can you do with the dryer lint?* When you dry your sweaters, you will end up with lots of colorful woolly dryer lint. This is fiber! What can you make with it? We've tried all kinds of projects, some of them involving white glue and flour, and we've made it into paper and beads and bowls. Dryer lint is a fun material to experiment with because it used to be part of your clothing, it's slightly different with every load, it's fuzzy — and it's free!

ARM WARMERS

This is a favorite felting project of ours because arm warmers are so cool! Also because we buy a lot of thrift-store sweaters for felting projects — and often the first thing we do is cut off the sleeves. That means we have a lot of sleeves lying around, which makes for a lot of material that we can use to make arm warmers, which, in turn, makes for a lot of excellent holiday gifts!

For a fun variation, you can make wristies instead: just cut the sleeves shorter, and flip them around so that the ribbing is at the wrist rather than at the fingers.

WHAT YOU NEED

- A felted wool or cashmere sweater (see page 83)
- Chalk
- Scissors
- Sharp needle
- Embroidery floss or sturdy thread

TIP ◤ FELTING WITH CASHMERE

Cashmere, which is a super-soft, expensive fiber, doesn't felt quite as well as most wool — but that's actually okay here, since a little bit of stretch isn't a bad thing, and the arm warmers aren't really inclined to unravel. Just make sure you're cutting up a discarded or thrifted sweater and not somebody's favorite wearable!

HOW YOU MAKE IT

1. Lay your arm down over the arm of the sweater, so that your fingers are on the cuff. Now decide how long you want your arm warmers to be — they can be wristies or run all the way to your elbow — mark the sleeve with chalk and cut. (The wrist end of the sweater sleeve will be the hand end of your arm warmer.) Cut the second sleeve the same way.

2. Lay the sleeve on your work surface and lay your hand on the sleeve. With chalk, mark along the arm seam (or fold if there's no seam) where you want the thumb hole. Line the second sleeve up with the first and mark a matching thumb hole.

3. Cut each thumb hole by making a very shallow moon shape. Try on the arm warmer and check that it's comfortable. If you need to, make the hole a little bigger; after being reinforced with stitching, it will be less stretchy.

4. Thread your needle (see page 15) with embroidery floss and knot the end (see page 16). Using buttonhole stitch (see page 37), sew around the edge of each thumbhole. Tie off the thread (see page 17) on the inside of the fabric and snip the thread.

If the arm warmers fit perfectly, voilà! You are done! If they feel too loose — and this is especially likely if you've made the wristies variation (see page 85), with the ribbing at the wrist rather than at the fingers — you can tighten them.

Turn one arm warmer inside out and put it on; then have a friend pinch the excess felt close to the edge of your hand or arm, and mark that line with chalk. Take off the arm warmer, pin along the chalk line, and with the needle and floss or sturdy thread, sew a running stitch (see page 33) or backstitch (see page 20) along the chalk line to make a new seam. Make sure to sew a few extra stitches at the beginning and end to reinforce the seam. Cut the excess fabric to within ½ inch of the seam.

Repeat on the second arm warmer or wristie.

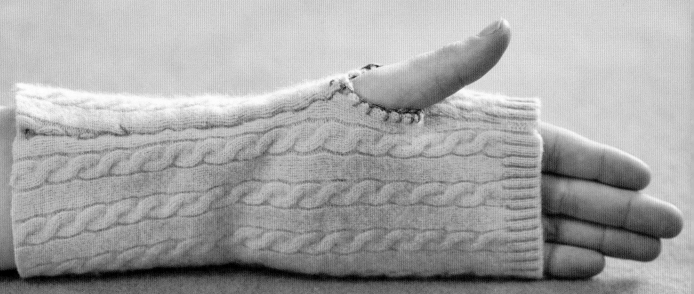

FANCY IT UP: FELT FLOWERS

To get your ideas flowering, leaf through a seed catalog or a wildflower field guide before starting. For each arm warmer, cut out one or more flower shapes from felt. (Using chalk or a fabric marker to sketch the shapes onto your felt might make the cutting easier).

Stitch your finished flowers to your arm warmers using the star variation of cross-stitch (see page 61) or treating each flower as if it were a shankless button with imaginary holes (see page 36).

You can also stack the shapes from largest to smallest, and stitch them together through their middles using several small running stitches (see page 33). To further decorate them, you can add a couple of beads or a button.

WE'RE NOT THE ONLY SPECIES THAT FELTS!

There's another type of felting called *needle felting*, which involves turning wool roving — soft unspun wool fibers — into fabric and objects by matting it together. The needle felter puts the wool fibers on a piece of foam and then pokes in and out with a special barbed needle that tangles the fibers just enough to stick them together. (If you really get into felting, you should ask for needle-felting supplies the next time you have a birthday coming up!)

Weirdly enough, there's a kind of wasp, the *Clistopyga*, that lays her eggs in a spider's web after paralyzing the spider. She then uses her long and barbed ovipositor (the egg-laying organ) to poke in and out of the silk to felt it,

thus sealing up the eggs, along with their first meal — the spider — in a protective cocoon.

Niclas Fritzén, an entomologist (a person who studies insects) writes, "The similarity with the human felting needle is striking, both concerning its structure and function, and it even serves the same purpose, namely to entangle fibres." Pretty cool, right?

FANCY THAT

Decorate your mittens by embroidering
designs on them! Or add beads or
buttons or appliqué on felt shapes or
flowers (see page 44).

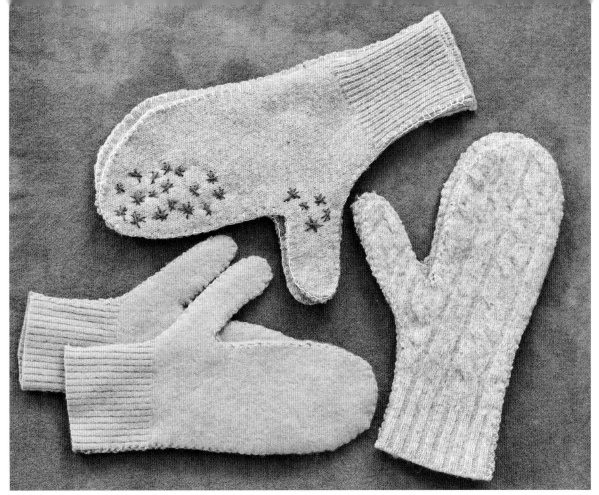

CUT-AND-SEW MITTENS

It's fun to wear (or gift) a pair of mittens you made yourself! And they can be as plain or as fancy as the sweater you felt. This is a super-easy project, since your own hand is the only pattern you need. And you don't even have to turn the fabric inside out, because you're going to blanket stitch around the outside of it! So take your time sewing, since your stitches will show.

WHAT YOU NEED

- Felted wool sweater with a ribbed waistband (see page 83)
- Chalk
- Straight pins
- Scissors
- Sharp needle
- Embroidery floss

HOW YOU MAKE THEM

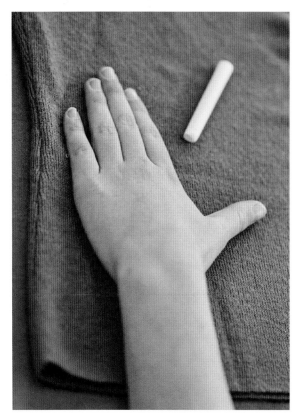

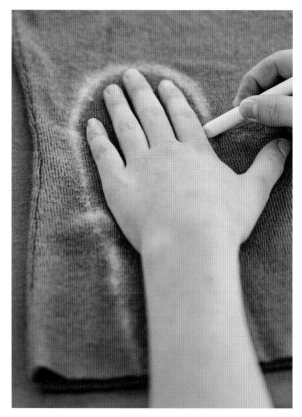

1. Keep the sweater right side out (the way you would wear it) and line up the front and back waistbands so that the ribbing is even along the bottom. Put your left hand on top of the sweater so that your wrist lies on top of the waistband, with the heel of your hand just above the ribbing's top edge.

   Do this as far to one side as you can, so that you can get two mittens out of the sweater.

2. Keep your fingers together and stretch your thumb out so that your left hand makes an L shape. Trace the outline of your hand and wrist with chalk, adding about ½ inch all the way around. This will give you plenty of room to sew your mitten together.

   If you're making the mitten for someone else, trace his or her hand. If it's a surprise, do your best with the sizing or use a mitten that person wears.

3. Pin through both layers to hold them in place, then cut the mitten shape out. Use this cutout shape to trace the mitten for the other hand. Pin along the outline, and cut the second mitten.

4. Thread your needle (see page 15) with embroidery floss and knot the end (see page 16). Starting from the wrist and with the knot inside the two layers, use the blanket stitch (see page 38) to sew the mitten together. Reinforce the seams along the wrist edges by stitching in one place a few times. Repeat with the other mitten.

Here's your finished mitten!

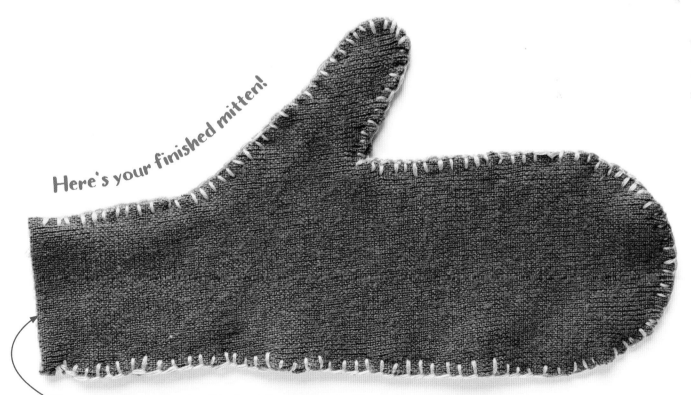

We used a sweater without a ribbed waistband, but our mitten came out great anyway!

MONSTER COIN POUCH

We love reaching into a monster's mouth to get out our moolah — and we're guessing you will, too! This is a fun, free-form project that lets you design your own pattern. If you don't want to make a coin pouch, you can skip the zipper and stuff the pouch with polyester filling (or felt scraps) to make a cute-and-scary stuffie!

WHAT YOU NEED

- A 4- or 5-inch zipper (see Note, page 98)
- Paper
- Pencil
- Scissors
- Felted wool (see page 83)
- Double-sided tape (optional)
- Straight pins
- Chalk or disappearing-ink fabric marker
- Sharp needle
- Sturdy thread or embroidery floss
- Buttons (or different-colored felt) for eyes

HOW YOU MAKE IT

1. Put your zipper on the paper, imagine it's a mouth, and, with a pencil, draw the shape of your monster face, leaving plenty of room around the zipper for cutting and sewing. Add ears and/or horns as you like. Cut out the pattern.

2. Stick the pattern to your felt with double-sided tape or pin it on with straight pins. Trace the pattern onto the felt with chalk or a fabric marker, then cut the shape out of the felt. Repeat, so that you have a front and a back. (If you're using thin felt, you can cut both pieces at the same time.)

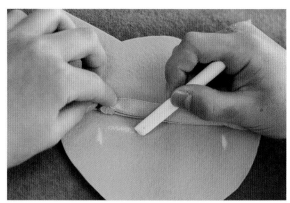

3. Pin the zipper to one of the cut pieces. With a fabric marker or chalk, mark a straight line along the zipper teeth where you want the mouth to go.

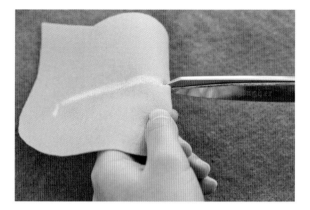

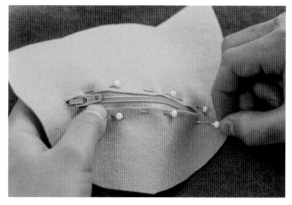

4. Cut a slit along the mouth line. This is easiest to do if you fold the fabric to make the first small cut.

5. Pin the zipper fabric to the underside of the felt so that just the zipper teeth poke through the slit out to the front.

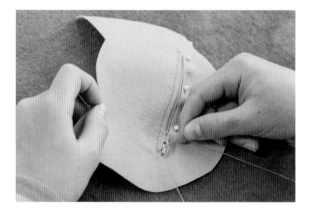

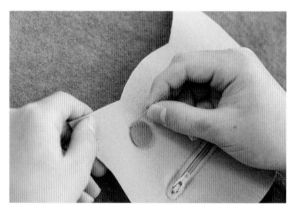

6. Thread your needle (see page 15) and knot the end (see page 16). Then sew together the top layer of the coin pouch and the fabric part of the zipper, using the backstitch (see page 20) all the way around.

You might find it hard to push your needle through the zipper fabric, but be patient! When you get back where you started, tie off the thread (see page 17) on the underside of the felt.

7. Sew on the button eyes (see page 34), if using, or cut circles from felt and sew them on using the whipstitch (see page 25).

GUESS WHAT?

A really expert sewer helped us with our green cat and used craft felt (instead of homemade felt) so you could see the process more clearly. That's why it looks so perfect! Don't worry — our stitches never look as neat as this. And yours don't have to, either.

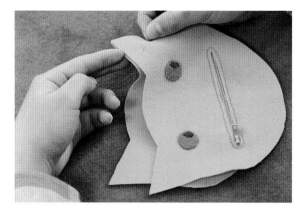 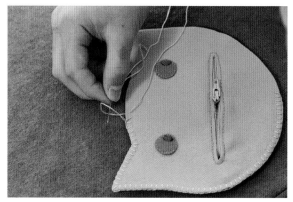

8. Line up the top and bottom pieces and pin them together.

9. Thread your needle with sturdy thread or embroidery floss and knot the end. Sew the two pieces together using either the blanket stitch (see page 38) or the whipstitch (see page 25). Tie off the floss (see page 17) and snip the end on the inside of the pouch.

NOTE:

You might be able to find a small zipper at your fabric store, where it will likely be called a "pocket zipper," but you can also easily order one online. Just type "4-inch zipper" into the search engine (or look on etsy.com). If anyone in your family has ruined a pair of pants recently, you could also try repurposing the zipper from the fly for this project!

SCRAP-FELT NECKLACE

We're always so in love with our own homemade felt that we can't bear to throw the scraps out. Luckily, we've figured out ways to use them! Like the flowers on page 89 and this cute necklace, that's as easy as cutting felt scraps into little squares and stringing them on a piece of embroidery floss or narrow elastic.

4

KNIT

Knitting is one of the many ways to turn a single strand of fiber into fabric; when you knit, you do that using two knitting needles. If you've ever had a beloved aunt or uncle knit you a sweater, you know what knitting looks like: even though the fabric seems like a solid thing, when you look closely at it, you can see the rows and rows of little stitches that went into making it. You might be surprised to look closely at other finer, smoother knit fabrics — a T-shirt, for example — and see that those, too, are made up of teeny-tiny stitches that are actually knit on a huge machine!

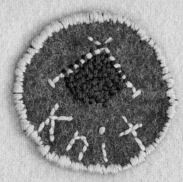

Knitting is a bit like riding a bike: it's a little tricky to learn, but once you do, you never forget how. (You might *think* you've forgotten, but once you have the knitting needles and yarn in your hands, it usually comes right back to you.) For us, the very best way to learn a skill like knitting is to find someone who knows how to knit.

But if you don't have a grandmother, uncle, friend, or babysitter who can help you in person, we've done our best to give you pictures and instruction that will help you learn. After you study our examples, you might even check out some online videos for a tiny bit more help. And even if you can ask an experienced knitter for advice, our how-to directions will still help you remember what to do when.

Be patient when you're learning, and try to remember that knitting takes time — even if you're excited to see your finished project. We like knitting in the winter, when we're cozy inside.

You'll see throughout this chapter that we specify different types and weights of yarn, and different sizes and thicknesses of knitting needles. But honestly? We've done a lot of knitting with whatever yarn and needles we found around the house! The main thing is to use needles that aren't too skinny, unless you want to spend a *looong* time on your knitting project. And use yarn you love, since you're going to be spending a lot of time with it.

GETTING STARTED

What You Need

Yarn. When you're just practicing, you can use any yarn at all. You may have some lying around from other craft projects, or you can ask your grandparents, uncle, or babysitter if they have any to spare. But for projects that are going to take a lot of time, it's nice to get wool or cotton yarn, or a fun or crazy yarn that feels special to you. Yarn is sold in *balls*, looser *skeins*, and looped bundles called *hanks*. It's also sold in different *weights*, which refers to the thickness of the strand and the size of the needle that you'd ideally use to knit it with. For each of the projects in this chapter, we'll give you yarn weight suggestions.

Knitting needles. These look like sharpened pencils (double-pointed needles have tips on both ends), and they can be made of wood, plastic, or metal. They come in lots of sizes and thicknesses: the most common range from US 1 (2.25 mm), the slenderest, to US 17 (12 mm), the thickest. If you're knitting with thinner yarn, ideally you'll want to use thinner needles; if you're using thicker yarn, pair it with thicker needles. As a rule, thicker needles will knit up your project more quickly than thinner ones will — so use thicker wool and needles if you're craving a speedy finish. In a pinch, you can sharpen ¼–inch dowels or chopsticks with a pencil sharpener and smooth them with sandpaper to make your own knitting needles.

Sharp wide-eyed sewing needle. Use a sharp needle with an eye that your yarn can fit through, for sewing up knitted projects that require it.

Circular knitting needles. These look like a pair of short knitting needles connected with a plastic or wire cord. They're for knitting around and around to create a tube shape, and we use them to knit the Cord-Slung Backpack on page 125 and the I-Cord Jump Rope on page 121.

Blunt-tipped wide-eyed needle. Use a dull needle with an eye that your yarn can fit through for weaving in the ends of your yarn.

Scissors. You'll need scissors for cutting your yarn, but it doesn't matter too much what kind they are, since it's not a lot of cutting.

Straight knitting needles

Tape measure or ruler. You might need one for measuring your projects as you work on them.

DID YOU KNOW? KNITTING IS *OLD*!

This Egyptian sock from around 400 CE shows an early form of knitting.

Our word *knit* comes from the Old English word for "knot": *cnyttan*. Long before the Middle Ages, though, people were knitting. For example, archaeologists in Egypt have found complicated knitted cotton socks that date back to 1000 CE — and they're thought to be the earliest example of knitting that we have. Many of the socks have Arabic blessings knit into them, as well as symbols to ward off evil.

HOW TO
WIND YARN INTO A BALL

Some yarn comes in a *ball* or in a looser *skein*, which makes life very easy, because you can knit directly from it! And some yarn comes in a *hank*, where it has been looped into a loose twist. If you try to knit from a hank, the yarn can get tangled, which is super frustrating!

To turn your hank into a ball, untwist it so that it's a big loop, and wrap it around the back of a chair, your own knees, or the outstretched arms of a patient friend. Where the yarn is tied together with little pieces of yarn, cut them.

Now find the end of the yarn and start winding it with one hand loosely around four fingers of your other hand. After you've made a little bundle of loops, slip

it off your hand and keep winding so that you're now wrapping the yarn around the middle of the bundle.

Rotate the ball as you wind so that it grows evenly; the bigger it gets, the easier it will be, and then you'll run out of yarn and be done. You might want to keep the ball in a tote bag or even a bowl while you're knitting, so it doesn't roll away and turn into an accidental cat toy!

HOW TO
MAKE A SLIP KNOT

A *slip knot* is a very basic first step in most knitting and crocheting projects. It creates a loop that can be tightened around the knitting needle or crochet hook.

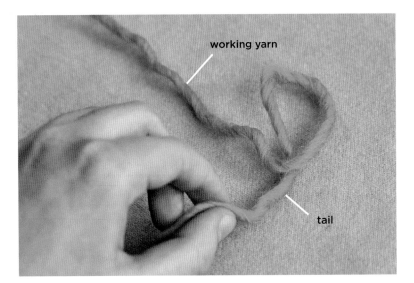

working yarn

tail

1. Make a loop with your yarn, leaving a tail about 6 inches long underneath the working yarn, which is the strand connected to your ball.

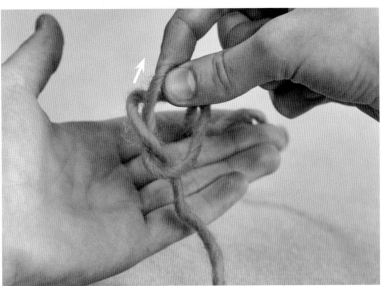

2. With your thumb and index finger, reach down through the loop and grab the working strand of yarn just below where it crosses the tail, pulling it up and through your original loop to create a new loop.

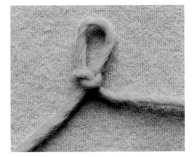

HOW TO
CAST ON

Casting on is making a first row of stitches on your needle, which will be the foundation of the rest of your knitting. There are many ways to cast on, and this is one of the easiest around. For this method, you will use only one knitting needle.

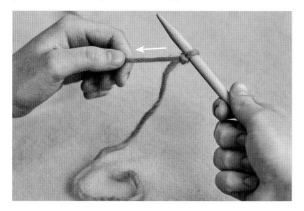

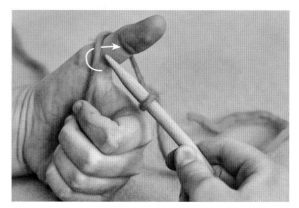

1. Make a slip knot (see page 106), then push your needle into the loop and tighten it (not too tight) by pulling the working yarn. Hold the needle in your right hand and the working yarn in your left hand.

2. Turn your left wrist so that the yarn coming from the needle loops over the top of your thumb. You'll be holding the working yarn against your palm with the fingers of your left hand. Hook the tip of the needle around the left side of the working yarn.

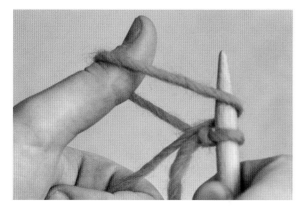

3. Push the tip of the needle up into the bottom of the loop you've made, between your thumb and your fingers.

4. Slide your thumb out and pull down with your left fingers to tighten the stitch (not too tight) onto the needle.

5. Repeat steps 2–4 until you have the number of stitches you need for your project.

HOW TO
KNIT ROWS

You've got your stitches cast on! Now it's time to _knit_. This kind of basic back-and-forth knitting creates a pattern called _garter stitch_, which makes a thick, stretchy fabric. We love how it looks.

1. Cast on (see page 107) however many stitches you need.

2. Hold the needle that has the cast-on stitches on it in your left hand, with the ball of yarn behind the needle. Hold the other needle in your right hand and push the tip of the right needle up through the bottom of the first stitch on the left needle from the front to the back. The two needles will cross, with the right needle behind the left one.

3. Using your left thumb and index finger, hold the needles together at the crossed point, and with your right hand, wrap the working yarn counterclockwise around the right needle, sliding it between the two needles so it comes out on the right, in front of the back needle.

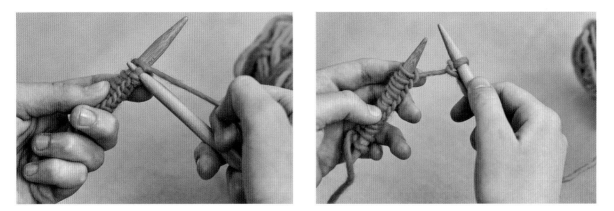

4. Holding both the right needle and the working yarn in your right hand, trace the tip of the right needle down the back of the left needle and up through the first stitch. This will put one stitch on your right needle. Use the right needle to push this stitch completely off the left needle. You've made a stitch! (It gets easier, honestly. Much, much easier.)

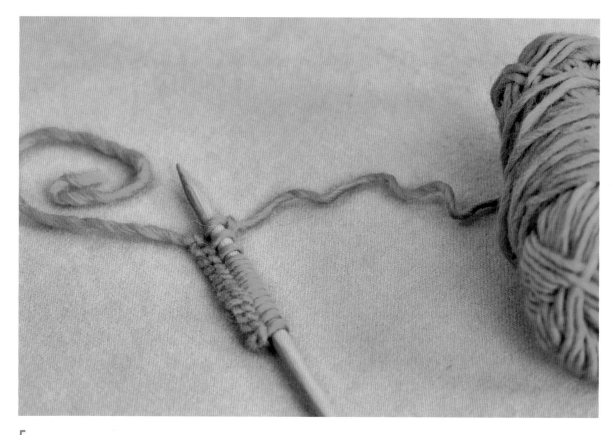

5. Repeat steps 2–4 to finish the row. Use your left hand as needed to push the stitches closer to the top of the needle as you work through the row.

At the end of the row, all of the stitches will be on the right needle. Simply move that needle into your left hand and the empty needle into your right hand, and start knitting another row!

The first row is the hardest, even for experienced knitters. Cast-on stitches can feel too tight or too loose, and it can seem like the project is going to look terrible. *Don't worry! The second row will be much better.*

TRY NOT TO (IF YOU CAN HELP IT)

. . . **PULL THE YARN TOO TIGHT** as you loop it, or it will get harder and harder to knit.

. . . **STOP KNITTING IN THE MIDDLE OF A ROW** — to help with the dishes or to get another handful of tortilla chips — because it's easy to get confused about where you left off. (Plus, now you have a handy procrastination technique! "In a minute!" you can yell. "As soon as I'm done with my row!")

. . . **PANIC** if all your stitches slide off the needle! Just thread the needle back through the dropped stitches as best you can and keep going.

HOW TO
CAST OFF

Also called *binding off*, this is the way you get your knitting off the needles at the end of the project without everything unraveling.

1. Knit the first 2 stitches in the row.

2. Use the tip of your left needle — or your left thumb and index finger — to pull the first stitch (farther from the needle tip) on the right needle . . .

. . . over the second stitch (closer to the needle tip) and then over the tip and off the needle completely. There will be only 1 stitch on the right needle.

3. Knit the next stitch.

4. Repeat steps 2 and 3 to the end of the row, at which point you will have only 1 stitch left on your needle.

5. Cut your working yarn, leaving a 6-inch tail. Slide your needle out of the stitch, leaving a loop. Thread the end of the tail into this loop, and pull gently to tighten.

WEAVE IN ENDS

Once you're done knitting (or crocheting) — or when you change colors in the middle of your project — you'll have loose ends of yarn dangling from your work.

Don't simply cut these ends off, since that will make everything more inclined to unravel. Just thread the end of the yarn onto a blunt wide-eyed sewing needle and weave in and out of the back of 3 or 4 nearby stitches, weaving twice in the last stitch. If there's still a little tail at that point, you can snip it off.

PHONE SWEATER

Stash your phone in a protective felted sleeve that's cool to boot. Or make a bigger one for your tablet by simply increasing the number of stitches you cast on and knitting a longer rectangle. (And if you are having too much fun knitting to stop? Nobody but you will know that your long scarf was supposed to have been a little pouch for your phone!)

WHAT YOU NEED

- Bulky-weight wool yarn (actual size shown above)
- Size 11 (8 mm) knitting needles
- Wide-eyed blunt sewing needle
- Scissors
- Access to a washing machine
- Embroidery floss (optional)
- Wide-eyed sharp sewing needle

BIG PICTURE

For a tablet about 7½ × 9½ inches, cast on 23 stitches and knit for 100 rows, or until the long side of your rectangle measures approximately 21 inches.

For a tablet about 5½ × 8 inches, cast on 17 stitches and knit for 86 rows, or until your rectangle is approximately 18 inches long.

TIP

GO FIGURE

Our instructions make a phone sweater that should fit a device that's about 3 x 5½ inches. If you're willing to experiment some, though, you can create a sleeve for any size phone or tablet (see our suggestions above).

Before you start, know that felting the fabric you knit can be nerve-racking — how small *will* it get? — and it's never an exact science. If you're knitting with thinner yarn or on bigger needles, it will shrink more. If it looks lacier or more open before you

wash it, it will likely shrink more as it tightens up. If you're a perfectionist, you're going to have to breathe and let go a little bit. (Good practice, right?)

Just remember that ultimately, before felting, you want a knitted rectangle that, when you fold it in half, is about ½ inch wider and about 1 inch longer than your device. In our instructions for a phone sleeve, your knitting before felting will be about 4 inches wide by 13 inches long.

HOW YOU MAKE IT

1. Cast on 12 stitches (see page 107).

2. Knit rows (see page 108) until your rectangle is about 13 inches long (for us this was 62 rows). Then cast off (see page 110) and weave in the ends with a blunt needle (see page 111).

3. To felt the fabric, toss it in your washer with a load of laundry that you're planning to do with a hot wash and cold rinse. Put your phone sweater in a pillowcase first, if you want to make sure it won't get caught on anything in the wash.

Lay the wet piece on a flat surface; arrange it into a nice, even rectangle; and let it air-dry. (This can take up to a day. Catherine just throws everything in the dryer, but this is not a recommended practice!)

When your felted fabric is completely dry, fold it in half with the short ends together. If the sleeve is still a little too big, just toss it back in the wash to tighten it up some more.

4. Thread your sharp needle (see page 15) with embroidery floss or yarn and, starting on the inside of the sleeve to hide the knot, use blanket stitch (see page 38) or whipstitch (see page 25) to sew up one of the long sides of the rectangle. Finish with the thread or yarn inside the sweater, tie off (see page 17), and trim the excess thread.

5. Repeat step 4 on the other long side of the phone sweater.

ADD A BUTTON

If your felted fabric is longer than you need, you can use the extra length to add a button (with or without a shank) for closing up the sleeve. When you fold the fabric before stitching the sides, just make sure you leave one side longer than the other, so that you can fold it down toward the button.

1. Thread a wide-eyed sharp-tipped needle with several inches of yarn. Starting on what will be the inside of the sleeve (the overhang), bring the needle through the middle of the very top of the fabric and back through the fabric again, right next to where it came out.

2. Pull the thread so that you leave a ½-inch loop (or however big you need it to fit around your button), then knot the two pieces of yarn together on the inside of the sleeve.

3. Fold the overhang down, like you're closing an envelope, and stretch the loop down until it's taut. Use chalk to mark where the bottom of the loop hits the front of the pouch.

4. Use strong thread or embroidery floss to sew on the button (see page 34) where you made your chalk mark. Close the pouch by folding over the flap and looping the yarn around the button.

HOW TO
CHANGE COLORS

If you want to change colors at any point, it's easy! We show making the swap at the beginning of a new row, but you can do it whenever you like.

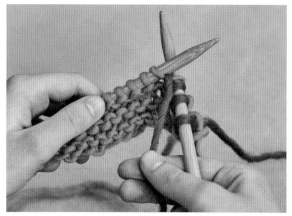

1. Hold the tails of the old yarn and new yarn together while you start knitting with the working yarn in your new color. After 3 or 4 stitches, the new color should be secure.

2. Snip the working yarn of the old color, leaving a tail about 6 inches long. You can weave this tail into the knitting at the end of your project (see page 111).

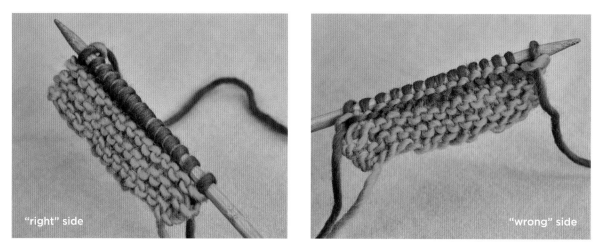

"right" side

"wrong" side

On one side of the finished fabric, the colors will be cleanly separated; on the other side, there will be two thin lines of alternating color between the two colors. Use whichever side you like best!

WHAT? VARIEGATED YARN

Variegated yarn is dyed with multiple colors, which results in color changes as you knit. It's so much fun to work with because your knitting automatically turns into colored stripes, without your doing anything to make it happen!

Also, if you are inclined to grow a little bored while knitting, the color change gives you something to look forward to. True, you're not, like, getting a horse or something — but maybe your favorite color is coming up, and that will be fun to knit with for a while! We especially love variegated yarn for long, narrow knitting projects — scarves, I-cords (see page 118), and even the Phone Sweater on page 112 — since the bands of each color are wider and more dramatic that way.

HOW TO
KNIT AN I-CORD

I-cord sounds like something you'd download from a tech website, but really it's just a skinny knitted tube that you can use for all kinds of things: a pair of shoelaces; a weird cozy for your pencil or the handle of a wooden spoon; a headband, bracelet, or belt; a decorative garland or a bow for a present; or a tube top or dress for your doll or stuffed animal!

If you've ever used a knitting spool or a Knitting Nancy, you basically made an I-cord — but we're going to teach you to make one using two double-pointed needles (if you have a pair of short, circular needles, you could use those instead). The weight of the yarn you use will depend on your project: you'll want to use fine yarn for shoelaces, for example, and bulky yarn for a jump rope.

TIP
WONDERING ABOUT WIDTH?

The more stitches you cast on (and the heavier your yarn), the bulkier your tube will be. If you're making something super narrow, like a shoelace, use the minimum number of stitches; if you're making something a bit wider, like a pair of leg warmers for a doll, cast on more stitches.

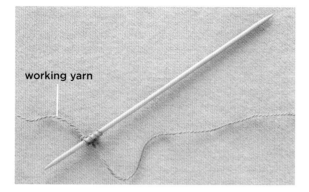

working yarn

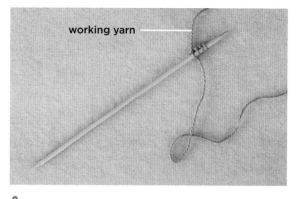

working yarn

1. Cast on 3 to 5 stitches (see page 107) or more, depending on what you need your I-cord for, and knit 1 row (see page 108). The working yarn is now closest to the left end of the needle in your right hand.

2. Move the needle with the knit stitches to your left hand and slide all the knitting to the right end of the needle. Bring the working yarn around the back of your knitting, from the left over to the right. With the empty needle in your right hand, knit another row as usual.

   Note: If you're using circular needles, when you're done knitting each row, slide the knitting right over the cable to the other needle tip.

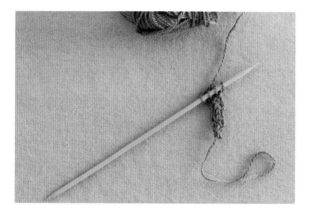

3. Repeat step 2, sliding your work from one end of the needle to the other after every row, and bringing the working yarn around from behind to knit the first stitch. At first, the tube will look a little open and messy, but it will get nice and tight as you knit.

4. When the cord is as long as you need it, cast off (see page 110) and weave in the loose ends (see page 111).

TIP ⟩ WHICH SIDE ARE YOU ON?

When you're knitting an I-cord, if you stop and need to know where you are, the needle with the knitting on it will be pointing to the right, and the working yarn should always be coming from the far left when you start the next row.

CRAFTING FOR GOOD

If you get super into fiber crafts, you might find yourself producing more hats, scarves, sweaters, blankets, and toys than you can gift to friends. There's a great solution: give them away. Lots of charitable organizations solicit useful goods from crafters for people in need: blankets for homeless people, stuffed animals for refugees, even superhero capes for kids living in shelters.

Catherine's daughter sewed baby hats for a hospital in Haiti, and she loved the feeling it gave her — the double-positive boost of making something *and* giving it away. We are loath to share website information in a book, given how quickly online information becomes outdated, but if you Google *crafting for charity*, you will find a number of websites looking for generous makers of things. Just be sure the website ends in ".org," so you know you're involved with a nonprofit organization.

I-CORD
JUMP ROPE

If you use T-shirt yarn (see page 178), it will make a really nice, heavy jump rope for skipping over. But you don't need to! Bulky-weight yarn will work, too. Just don't use leftovers from the baby slippers your mom was knitting: that yarn will be too thin and light, and it will take forever to knit.

WHAT YOU NEED

- Bulky-weight yarn (actual size shown above) or T-shirt yarn
- Circular or double-pointed knitting needles (the shortest and thickest ones you have)
- Scissors

Our tall friend here needs to keep knitting.

HOW YOU MAKE IT

1. Cast on 3 stitches (see page 107), then knit an I-cord (see page 118) that's long enough to swing and jump over: hold both ends in your hands and step on the bottom arch; the ends should reach almost to your armpits. If you want to change colors, just tie on a new strand of yarn and weave the ends in (see page 111).

2. Cast off (see page 110), then weave in the ends (see page 111) and skip away!

TRY THIS

If you're not a jumper, consider
knotting your rope and sling-
ing it across your shoulders,
messenger-bag style, then use
clips or carabiners to hang water
bottles and a pocket knife (and
whatever else you need) on your
next hike or outing.

CORD-SLUNG BACKPACK

You'll make this useful pack "in the round," which means knitting it as a tube on circular needles. Think of all the tubes you could knit once you learn this method! Leg warmers or arm warmers, or a cozy for your neck or water bottle. We'll also show you how to tweak this backpack to make a really simple hat — with pom-poms! — in the variation that follows.

After knitting the main part of the bag, you'll knit and felt an I-cord, which does double duty as a button-loop fastener and strap.

WHAT YOU NEED

- Bulky-weight yarn (actual size shown above)
- US size 11 (8 mm) 16-inch (40 cm) circular knitting needle (Longer needles won't work for this project.)
- Scissors
- Wide-eyed sewing needle
- Access to a washing machine
- Button to close the bag
- Smaller-eyed sewing needle
- Embroidery floss

TIP ▶ STRAIGHT LACED

If you only have straight needles, you can still make this project: knit a rectangle by casting on half the number of stitches you would for the tube. Keep knitting until the rectangle is twice as long as we call for in the tube instructions, then fold the rectangle in half and stitch up the sides.

HOW YOU MAKE IT

BAG

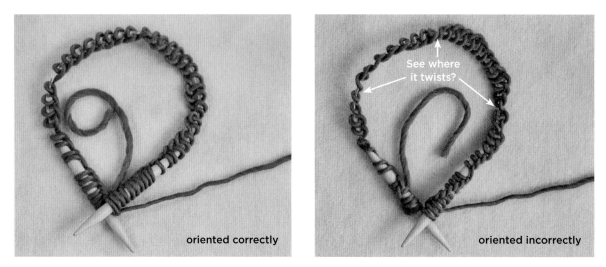

oriented correctly

See where it twists?

oriented incorrectly

1. Cast on 52 stitches (see page 107) or if you're using yarn that's not bulky weight, adjust accordingly: for thinner yarn, cast on additional stitches; for thicker yarn, cast on fewer stitches.

    Arrange the cast-on stitches so they are all oriented in the same direction and not twisting around the needles. This will prevent you from making a twisted circle, or Möbius, when you join your stitches. (If, as you knit, you find that you *have* accidentally created a twist, search the Internet for *how to fix a twist circular knitting* and watch a video about it. It's actually not too hard to fix!)

working yarn

2. Hold the needles so the working yarn is on the right-hand needle, then insert the right needle into the first stitch on the left needle (the first stitch you cast on) and knit (see page 108) as usual. This creates a continuous circle of stitches.

3. Knit knit knit knit. Instead of ending straight rows and switching the needles from hand to hand, you will simply knit around and around, continuously, creating a tube. Listen to an audiobook or your favorite podcast. Talk to your friends.

   This is called *knitting meditation* because once you get into the groove, you don't really have to think at all. Shake your hand out when it gets crampy, and add another color at some point if you want, but the stitch never changes.

4. Keep knitting until the backpack seems long enough to hold the things you'll likely put in it. Ours is about 10 inches long, which was 43 rows.

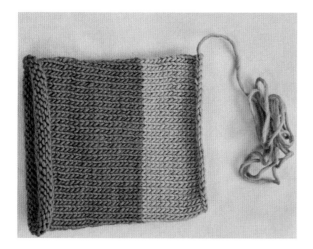

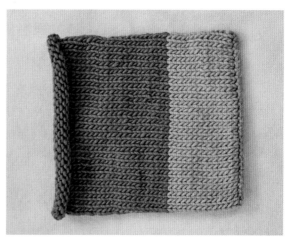

5. Cast off (see page 110), leaving about an arm's length of yarn attached before you cut your working yarn. Now you have a tube!

6. Thread the attached yarn from step 5 into the wide-eyed sewing needle. Stitching in place a few times for security at the beginning and end of the row, sew up the end of the tube using a whipstitch (see page 25).

   Weave the ends into the back of the fabric (see page 111), starting and ending on the inside so the knots won't show.

BUTTON-LOOP FASTENER AND STRAP

1. Cast on 5 stitches. Knit an I-cord (see page 118) that's about 60 inches long, then cast off (see page 110). Ideally you'll use the same weight of yarn as for the bag, but you can use any color.

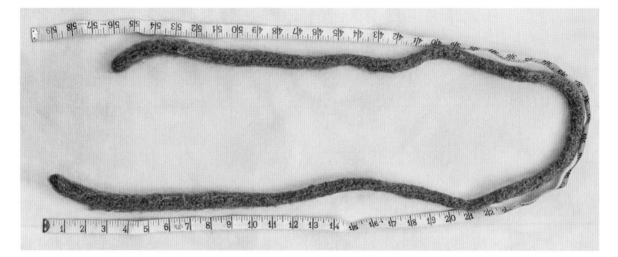

2. Felt the I-cord in the washing machine (see page 83) putting it in a pillowcase so it doesn't tangle around everything in the load. Then air-dry it by hanging it over your shower rod.

We've found that an I-cord usually shrinks in length by about a third when you felt it: when we felted a 60-inch I-cord, for example, we ended up with a 40-inch felted strap.

3. Fold the felted I-cord in half and make a loop big enough to fit around your button; position the button loop at the top of the bag and pin it in place. Thread the smaller-eyed sewing needle with embroidery floss (see page 15) and knot the end (see page 16).

4. Starting from the inside of the bag so your knot won't show, insert the needle through the center of one of the bag's open edges, then into one side of the I-cord. Sew back through the other side of the I-cord and back into the bag.

   Repeat this process twice more, so you have 3 stitches firmly connecting the I-cord and the bag. Tie the embroidery floss on the inside of the bag (see page 17), and snip off the excess.

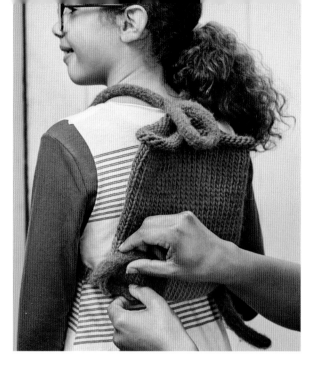

5. Use your fingers to push the end of each strap through both layers of the backpack at the corner so that the cord emerges on the front side of the front layer (where the button will be).

6. Measure the straps on the person who will be wearing the backpack. You want it to be easy to get the bag on and off without having the straps so long that they easily slip off the shoulders. Knot the cord close to the pack to keep the straps the right length. If you need to make it shorter, snip off the excess I-cord. (It's felted, so it shouldn't unravel.)

   Repeat with the other side, making sure it's the same length as the first strap.

7. Use embroidery floss to sew the button on at the top center of the front of the pack (see page 34). Knot the floss on the inside of the pack.

GET A (DIFFERENT) HANDLE

To make a simpler shoulder bag, skip adding a button and after step 2, attach the I-cord to the two sides of the bag's opening. Or, for either type of bag, skip the I-cord and instead use a 40-inch length of nylon or cotton strapping (the strong, ribbon-like material you make belts or straps out of) or nylon climbing rope.

TUBE HAT
WITH
POM-POMS

To make a hat instead of a backpack,
work the directions from pages
126 and 127 through Bag step 6 —
casting off and sewing up when the
tube seems like it's the right length
for a hat. (Try it on as you go!)
This will be the body of your hat.

POM-POMS

1. Thread a 10-inch piece of yarn between the
   center tines of a fork, and hold one end down
   along the handle of the fork.

2. Wrap a new piece of yarn around the tines
   75 (or so) times to form a bundle, then cut
   the wrapping yarn.

3. Bring the two tails of the original 10-inch length up and over the bundle without removing the bundle
   from the fork, and tie them together very tightly. Trim the ends.

4. Slide the blade of a pair of scissors into the loops on the back of the fork and carefully snip through all the loops. Fluff up the pom-pom and trim any stray longish ends.

5. Thread a wide-eyed needle with a new piece of yarn, about 10 inches long, then work the needle through both layers of one corner of the hat. Push the needle up through the pom-pom, knot the ends of the yarn together, and snip off the excess.

6. Repeat steps 1–5 for the other side of the hat.

FOR FUN

PROLIFIC POM-POMS

You can use puffy pom-poms in plenty of other ways: decorate your skate laces, adorn a barrette or headband, or fancy up your bookmark or ukulele strap! Embellish pillow corners, wrapped gifts, or your Christmas tree. Or make a garland to decorate your room — just thread a length of yarn onto a needle and push it right through the pom-poms to string them up.

YARN BOMBING!

Yarn bombing, also known as *guerrilla knitting* or *graffiti knitting*, is a kind of street art made by knitters and crocheters who cover unlikely objects and surfaces — telephone poles, tree trunks, benches, and bridges — with their colorful craft. As yarn bombers see it, everything is better with a nice cozy. The art is practiced worldwide, and while it's technically illegal in some places, all it takes to remove the yarn is a pair of scissors!

CROCHET

When you crochet, you use a single hooked needle to turn yarn into chained loops that link together to form a piece of fabric. There are some very traditional forms of the craft: if you've ever seen a lace tablecloth, for example, or a granny-square afghan — which is a kind of blanket pieced together from lacy squares — chances are you've seen the results of crochet.

135

But the thing is, no matter how old or traditional a craft it is, it's ours to learn and use however we like! That means we can make wrist cuffs and neck cozies, if we want to, or bead bracelets, leg warmers, or weird monster creatures. In fact, crochet is an art that is really coming back in style. People are doing it a lot these days, and they're making anything they can imagine.

One thing that makes crocheting different from knitting — besides using one hook instead of two needles — is that you start and finish one stitch at a time. When you're knitting, on the other hand, you keep an entire row of stitches open, and if you've ever had a knitting needle slide out from the project you're working on, you understand the related danger of this method. Crochet is also, as you get more experienced, uniquely easy to work into rounds (think lace doilies or Hacky Sacks) and odd shapes (think cactus, amoeba, or coral reef), whereas knitting lends itself more easily to rectangles and tubes.

But we're just going to get you started here. We'll show you the basics, but don't let your lesson end with these pages! Tuck a crochet hook and a small ball of yarn into your backpack in case, when you least expect it, you end up in the company of an expert crocheter! He or she will have so much to teach you.

If you're left-handed, crocheting might seem tricky at first. For some tips, see Hey, You Left-Handed Lovies! (page 7).

GETTING STARTED

What You Need

Yarn or thread. We're big fans of using whatever odds and ends of yarn you find around the house, but if someone is taking you yarn shopping, here's our advice: when you're first learning to crochet, a nice, smooth, light-colored yarn is easiest, because you'll be able to see your stitches. We like to use wool or a wool blend, since it has a little bit of stretch that makes it easier for beginners to work with.

Yarn is sold in *balls*, looser *skeins*, and loose bundles called *hanks*. (See page 105 to learn how to turn a hank into a ball — a very useful step before you start crocheting with the yarn.)

As you get more practiced, you might like to use *perle cotton*, which is a little shiny and is perfect for crochet. It's often sold in *cones* or *tubes*, but sometimes comes in hanks. (To prevent the hank from becoming tangled, see Storing Your Embroidery Floss, page 51.)

Crochet hook. Like knitting needles, crochet hooks are made of different materials, including metal,

plastic, and wood, and come in different sizes, which are named with both letters and numbers: the skinnier the hook, the lower the letter and number (a US C/2 [2.75 mm] hook, for example, is much slimmer than an L/11 [8 mm]). Do you feel like we just taught you calculus by accident? Don't worry. The gist of it is that you'll use a thicker crochet hook with thicker yarn, and a thinner one with thinner yarn. Unlike knitting needles, you use only one crochet hook at a time!

Scissors. You'll need scissors for cutting your yarn, but it doesn't matter too much what kind they are, since it's not a lot of cutting.

Tape measure or ruler. You'll need one for measuring your projects as you work on them.

Blunt-tipped wide-eyed needle. Use a dull needle with an eye that your yarn can fit through for weaving in the ends of your yarn and sewing up projects that require it.

CROCHET CONFESSION

Do you know the theater expression "breaking the fourth wall"? The *fourth wall* is the imaginary boundary separating the audience and the actions on the stage. When actors "break" through it, they address the audience directly and remind you that what you're watching is a play. Right now, you're not watching a play, and we're not actors, but we're going to remind you that this is a book being written by two actual people. Because here's a secret: we started writing it without actually knowing how to crochet!

We've both been doing fiber crafts for most of our lives, and we both taught all our kids to knit and sew and felt and embroider and weave. But somehow neither of us had ever learned how to crochet. *And we were nervous about learning it!*

"Do you think we really need a chapter on crochet?" we asked our editor, and she said, "Yes. We really need a chapter on crochet." So we learned how to crochet. We had to read books and watch videos and get help from our friend Sara Delaney, who used to work at our local yarn store and who literally wrote the book *How to Crochet*. And little by little, we got the hang of it.

We're not telling you this to make you nervous about crochet. Just the opposite, actually. We're telling you this so you understand that all of these fiber crafts are skills that you really *can* learn, even if you haven't already been doing them for your whole life. Some of them might be easy for you, and some might be harder, but you just have to be patient and practice, practice, practice.

And guess what? Now Nicole loves to crochet! Catherine is still learning. But she's working on it, and she's getting better. She really is.

CROCHETING IS *OLD*!

Crochet is an old French word that comes from the German word *croc*, which means "hook." In the seventeenth century, crochet described a form of making lace, as well as the hooked needle that was used to do it. Both are still used today, 400 years later!

This Irish lace handkerchief was crocheted in the nineteenth century.

FOR FUN

FINGER CROCHET

Crocheting with your fingers instead of a hook is a good method to start with because it introduces you to the basic process in a simple way. Try finger-crocheting shoelaces, a bracelet, or a hair tie. Or tie a length of it into a bow to pretty up a gift! These instructions teach you how to make a finger-crocheted chain, but if you like the process, keep experimenting; you can also make more complicated crochet stitches — and projects — using just your fingers.

1. Make a slip knot at the end of the yarn (see page 106), leaving a 6-inch tail.

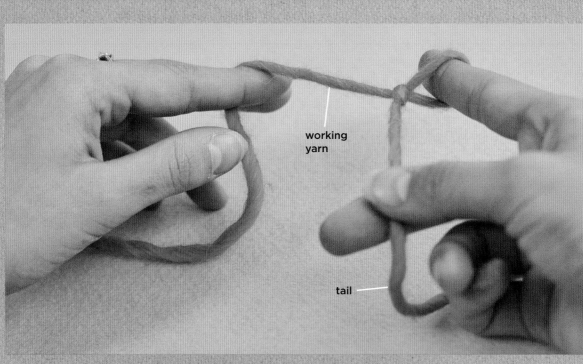

working yarn

tail

2. Push your right index finger into the loop formed by the slip knot, and tighten it slightly, but leave enough room to reach your right thumb through as well. Hold the working yarn in your left hand.

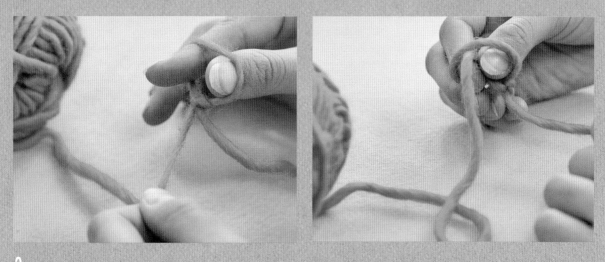

3. With your right thumb and index finger, reach through the loop, grab the working yarn, and bring it through the original loop to create a new loop.

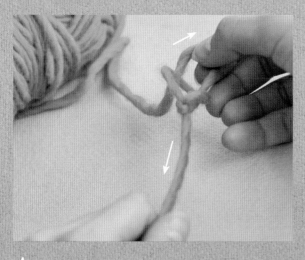

4. Adjust the tightness of the chain by gently pulling the new loop and the tail in opposite directions.

5. Repeat steps 3 and 4 until the chain is as long as you like, then snip the yarn, leaving a 6-inch tail. Thread the tail through the last loop and pull it tight.

HOW TO
CHAIN STITCH

The *chain stitch* is the basis for the crochet projects in this chapter, so you'll want to practice it for a little while before moving on to more exciting things. You might rip it out (that means pull the working yarn to undo the stitches) and start over again. Otherwise use your finished chain to tie something up — like a present or your hair — or to make a leash for your cat (because cats love that!). When we refer to using this stitch, we will use the verb *chain*, as in "chain 10 stitches, then . . ."

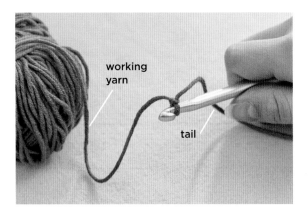

1. Make a slip knot at the end of the yarn (see page 106), leaving a 6-inch tail. Insert the crochet hook into the loop and pull on the tail to tighten the loop around the hook, being careful to not pull it too tight! The working yarn — attached to the ball — should be trailing off to the left, and the tail will be to the right (you'll weave it into the project at the end).

2. Hold the hook in your right hand, like it's an ice cream scoop. Hold the working yarn in your left hand and the tail between your left thumb and middle finger. It will feel awkward at first, like you need a third — or fourth — hand. Hang in there!

With the hook facing you, wrap the working yarn over the hook from the back to the front. (This action will sometimes show up in the projects as the instruction *yarnover*.)

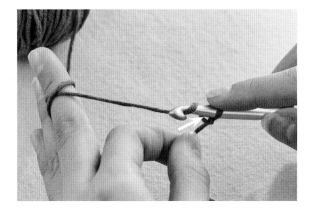

3. Catch the working yarn inside the tip of the hook, then turn the hook downward slightly, about a quarter turn, and use the hook to pull the working yarn through the first loop that's already on the hook. You've now completed a chain stitch!

4. Repeat steps 2 and 3 over and over to create a chain of any length, or just to practice. When you are done, snip the working yarn and pull that tail through the final loop. (If this is the beginning, or foundation, chain for a bigger crochet project, you won't tie off or cut the working yarn at this point.)

TRY THIS

KEEP THE DISTANCE BETWEEN YOUR HANDS more or less the same as you crochet.

REMEMBER TO TURN YOUR HOOK so it's facing down before pulling the working yarn through the loop.

IF YOUR STITCHES ARE TOO SMALL to work into easily, you may be pulling your yarn too tight. Try relaxing your hands a little bit. Sliding each newly completed stitch down the hook an inch or so before starting your next stitch can also help keep your stitches a little looser.

REMEMBER TO WRAP the yarn *from back to front*.

TO KEEP YOUR CHAIN FROM TWISTING, move your left hand up the chain as you work, so your thumb and middle finger will hold the dangling chain instead of the original tail. This will help keep the edges of your finished crocheted projects straight.

BEADED CHAIN BRACELET

This project is a perfect first foray into crocheting. It relies entirely on the first two steps of any crochet project: the slip knot and the chain stitch. Once you master the chain stitch, you can whip up yards and yards of chain in no time at all, so all of your friends can get a stylish and simple bracelet to wear.

Oh, and by the way, if you want this to wrap around your wrist more times — or if you want a necklace instead or even some ankle jewelry — just start with more beads and make the chain as long as you like!

WHAT YOU NEED

- Sewing needle with an eye wide enough for the thread to fit through but narrow enough to fit through the beads and buttonholes
- Perle cotton (we use size 5; actual size shown above)
- 18 beads with a hole big enough for the sewing needle to go through (6/0 [4 mm] beads work well)
- Crochet hook (we use US C/2 [2.75 mm])
- Scissors
- Button

TIP ◄ CHOOSING YOUR BUTTON

Use a button that fits very snugly through the loop made at the beginning of the chain in step 3 (page 146). You really want it to just barely squeeze through!

HOW YOU MAKE IT

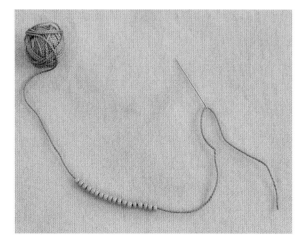

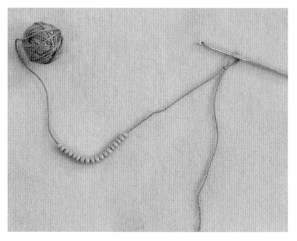

1. Thread the needle onto the end of your perle cotton thread (don't cut the thread) and string on all the beads. Slide the beads down the string at least 6 inches.

    Note: If you aren't sure how long your bracelet needs to be when you start, thread a few extra beads just in case. You don't have to use them if you don't need them, but you can't easily add beads later if you find you want a longer bracelet.

2. Remove the needle and make a slip knot on the end of the thread (see page 106), leaving a 6-inch tail. Insert the crochet hook and pull gently on the working thread to tighten it.

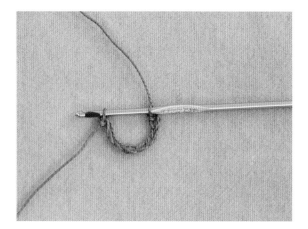

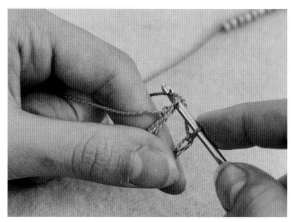

3. To make a loop for the button closure, chain 10 (see page 142), then shape the chain into a loop. Insert the hook into the first stitch of the chain. *You now have* 2 loops on the hook.

4. Yarnover, and pull the hook back through both loops. Now you're ready to chain stitch with beads!

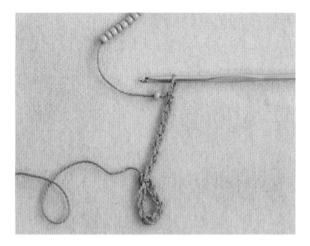

5. Chain 10. Slide a bead down to just above the last stitch made, then chain 6 more times. You will more or less ignore the bead, which will be locked in place by the next stitch in the chain.

6. Continue to add a bead, chain 6, and add a bead until the entire chain gets long enough to wrap around your wrist (or the wrist of your lucky friend) three times. End with a chain 6 (or more, if you need more length), then snip the thread and pull it through the final chain, leaving a 6-inch tail.

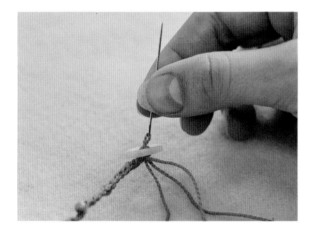

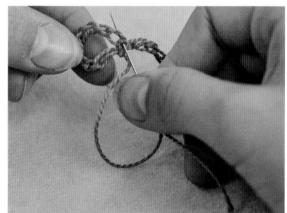

7. To finish the button closure, thread the tail into the needle (see page 15) and use it to sew the button in place (see page 34). If you're using a shank button, bring the needle and thread through the shank a few times; if it is a button with several holes, secure it well through the holes.

Stitch the button down into the chain a few times, making sure it is really secure, then tie off the thread on the underside of the button (see page 17). Weave the tail into a few stitches near the button, and snip the excess thread.

8. Finally, thread the needle with the tail hanging from your initial slip knot. Weave it down and back up into the beginning of the chain a few times, then snip off the excess thread.

HOW TO
SINGLE CROCHET

Now that you've mastered the crochet chain, you're ready to crochet an actual piece of fabric. There are many crochet stitches, but *single crochet* is a simple back-and-forth that makes a sturdy, even fabric — perfect for the projects that follow.

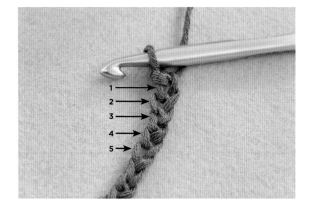

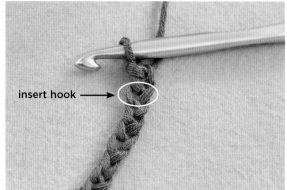

1. Chain (see page 142) however many stitches you need, plus 1. (For example, if you want your piece to be 5 stitches wide, chain 6 stitches. The loop on your hook **never** counts as a stitch. This is more important than it might seem!) Your initial chain is called the *foundation chain*.

2. Hold the chain so that the side that looks like a line of Vs is facing you. (This is the *front*; the *back* has small bumps down the middle of the chain.) Insert the tip of the hook, from front to back, through the top strand of the second chain away from the hook.

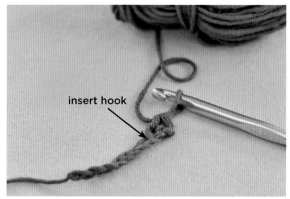

3. Yarnover and pull the yarn back through the top strand of the second chain from the hook. *You now have* 2 loops on your hook.

4. Yarnover again and pull the hook through the 2 loops on the hook, which will leave you with 1 loop on the hook. Insert the hook into the top strand of the chain stitch immediately to the left of the stitch you just made.

5. Repeat steps 3 and 4 the entire length of the chain.

6. Begin the next row by turning your work over from right to left (think of it like a book page), and make 1 chain stitch, just like when you were making the foundation chain. This extra stitch is called a *turning chain*.

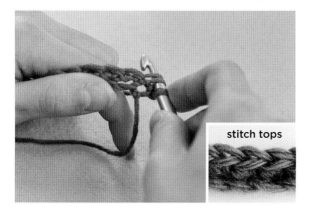

stitch tops

7. You will be looking at the back of the stitches you just made. Notice the two strands of yarn — like two legs forming a V shape — at the top of each stitch. Insert the tip of the hook under both of these strands in the first stitch.

   Complete your single crochet stitch just as you did when working into the foundation chain: yarnover, pull the yarn through to create 2 loops, yarnover, and pull through both loops.

8. Repeat step 7 to the end of the row. Finish the row by turning your work over from right to left and making another turning chain as in step 6. You are now ready to single crochet the next row.

HOW TO
CHANGE COLORS

Making stripes in your crocheting is easy!

1. On the last stitch before you want your new color to start, yarnover and pull through one loop.

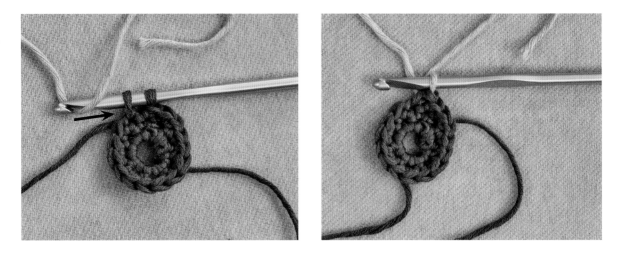

2. Pick up your new color, yarnover, and pull through two loops with the new color. You are now ready to crochet normally with the new color.

3. Leaving a 6-inch tail, cut off the old color and weave in the loose end (see page 111), or leave the old color attached and pick it up again later if you want to alternate the colors.

PENCIL ROLL

We're suckers for a roll-up of pencils arranged in rainbow order! And it's just so handy for art on the go. Don't worry: this project may look complicated, but it's really just a straightforward rectangle of crochet. Of course, if you prefer, you could make this pouch for a different purpose: to hold your crochet supplies, say — hooks and scissors and such — or for your toothbrush, toothpaste, and comb when you're away from home. Just size the channels accordingly to fit whatever you want to store and carry.

- Medium-weight cotton yarn (We use worsted or DK, which is a little thinner than worsted; actual size shown above.)
- Crochet hook (We use US F/5 [3.75mm].)
- A pencil (or whatever you're planning to keep in the roll) for size reference
- Scissors
- Wide-eyed sewing needle

HOW YOU MAKE IT

ROLL

1. Make a slip knot in the end of the yarn (see page 106), leaving a 6-inch tail. Insert the crochet hook and chain 25 stitches (see page 142). The finished chain should be about one and a half times the length of a standard pencil or whatever you plan to keep in your roll. You can undo some chain stitches to make it shorter or add some chain stitches to make it longer.

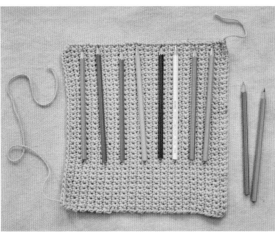

2. Single crochet (see page 148) until the rectangle is wide enough to fit all the pencils you want to store. Test this by placing the pencils on top of the rectangle with ½-inch spaces between them. Leave an arm's length of working yarn attached.

3. Fold up the bottom 4 inches of the rectangle to create the pocket for the pencils. Thread the working yarn through the sewing needle, then close up one side of the rectangle from the top to the bottom with the running stitch (see page 33) or whipstitch (see page 25). Do not cut your yarn yet!

4. Slide a pencil (or whatever you will carry in your roll) into the folded pocket, as close to the stitched-up edge as possible, to use as your guide to make sure your channels are wide enough.

Push the needle into the folded end of the fabric, then bring it back up through the fabric at the bottom edge about 3 stitches in from the side edge, or whatever distance you need to make your pencil fit snugly.

5. Use a running stitch to sew from the bottom fold to the top edge of the pocket, making sure you go through both pieces of fabric. You can use your crocheted stitches as a guide to keep your line of stitches straight.

starting tail

6. Poke your needle up through the top edge and blanket stitch (see page 38) or whipstitch another pencil width over across the pocket edge. I hen use a running stitch to sew back down the folded fabric from top to bottom for the second pencil.

7. Bring the needle up through the fabric another pencil width over, then repeat steps 5 and 6 until you get to the other edge of the roll. If the last channel you stitch ends up being the wrong size, use it for two pencils or for a special super-skinny pencil. Weave in the working yarn and starting tail (see page 111), and cut them.

TIE

1. To create a tie for your roll, insert your hook into the edge of a stitch about halfway up one short side of the finished rectangle. With a fresh length of working yarn, yarnover and pull your hook back through the edge stitch. *You now have* 1 loop on your hook.

    From here, chain (see page 142) a tie long enough to wrap once around the rolled case, about 6 inches. Knot your chain tightly at the end and snip the working tail.

> **TIP**
>
> ## BE SQUARE
>
> If your rectangle of crocheted fabric is looking more like a triangle or trapezoid, you are probably unintentionally skipping stitches at the ends of the rows. Almost everyone does this when they first start crocheting. To prevent it, use your crochet hook to pull a scrap piece of a different-colored yarn through the first and last stitches of each row and leave them there. This way, you won't miss working into those stitches when you come back to them.

2. Repeat step 1 to make a second chain coming out of the same side stitch.

3. Weave in the starting ends of both chains (see page 111), then wrap up your roll and tie a bow!

HOW TO
INCREASE CROCHET STITCHES

There are lots of ways to add stitches when you're crocheting, and each method will do something different to the fabric you're creating. To make the bowl shape you'll need for creating the Hacked Sack (page 157), you'll work 2 single crochet stitches into certain stitches of the ring. Don't worry — we'll tell you when you need to do this! And here's how.

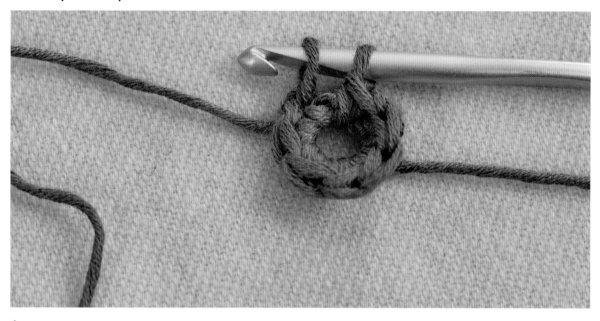

1. Insert the hook into the first stitch from the previous round and single crochet.

first single crochet

second single crochet

2. When your first single crochet stitch is complete, insert the hook again into the same stitch you just crocheted into. Single crochet.

DECREASE CROCHET STITCHES

There are many ways to decrease stitches when you're crocheting, but all of them result in making your fabric narrower. When making the Hacked Sack (page 157), you will decrease stitches to close up the ball. In this *single crochet decrease*, you will crochet 2 stitches together, ending up with 1 stitch. The advantage to this method is that it doesn't leave a hole in your fabric — which is especially helpful when you're filling that fabric with popcorn or beans!

1. Begin your single crochet stitch as normal: insert your hook under both strands of the next stitch and yarnover. Pull through; *you now have* 2 loops on your hook.

2. Insert the hook into the next stitch, yarnover, and pull through. *You now have* 3 loops on your hook.

3. Yarnover and pull your hook through all 3 loops. *You now have* just 1 stitch on your hook and have completed a *single crochet decrease*.

HACKED SACK

You might be more familiar with the brand name Hacky Sack! But whatever you call it, if you have a small footbag or sack, you always have a game to play — with one other person, a group, or even by yourself. Why not crochet one and keep it in your backpack?

Yes, this is the most advanced crochet project here, but you really can do it. And think how proud you'll be when someone says, "Dude, cool Hacky Sack! Where'd you get it?" And you can shrug and say, "Oh, this old thing? I made it."

WHAT YOU NEED

- Medium-weight cotton yarn (We use worsted or DK, which is a little thinner than worsted; actual size shown above.)
- Crochet hook (We use US F/5 [3.75 mm].)
- Stitch marker (see page 159)
- Popcorn kernels or dried beans
- Funnel (optional)
- Scissors
- Blunt wide-eyed sewing needle

HOW YOU MAKE IT

SETUP

Make a slip knot (see page 106), leaving a 6-inch tail, and insert the crochet hook.

1. Chain 4 (see page 142). Insert the hook into the first chain stitch.

2. Yarnover and pull through both loops on the hook. This connects the circle so that you can crochet around and around, which is called (wait for it!) *crocheting in the round.*

3. There should be an empty place in the middle of the circle, like the hole in a donut.

CROCHETING THE SACK

Work second single crochet into the same hole.

ROUND 1: Chain 1, then work 6 single crochet stitches (see page 148) into the hole. There is now a ring made of 6 stitches.

ROUND 2: Work 2 single crochet stitches into each stitch in the ring (see page 155). At the end of this round, you will have 12 stitches in the circle.

ROUND 3: Work 2 single crochet stitches in the first stitch of the previous round and 1 single crochet into the next stitch. Repeat — alternating between working 2 stitches (A) then 1 stitch (B) into each stitch from the previous row — until you get to the end of the round. *You now have* 18 stitches total.

ROUND 4: Work 2 single crochet stitches into the first stitch and 1 single crochet into the next 2 stitches. Repeat the 2-1-1 sequence until you get to the end of the round. *You now have* 24 stitches total, and your fabric will start to make a bowl shape! (This is good.)

Once the fabric begins to form a bowl, push it so it becomes a bowl going in the opposite direction — like you're turning a hat inside out — and continue crocheting.

ROUNDS 5-9: Work 1 single crochet stitch all the way around for five rounds. There are no increases in these rounds, which we did with blue yarn, but you need to count the rounds.

TIP

USING STITCH MARKERS

Even the most experienced knitters and crocheters need help keeping track of their stitches. Craft stores sell fancy stitch markers, but you also can use something you have lying around the house, like a safety pin, a paper clip, or a little loop of a different-colored yarn. When crocheting a circle, place a stitch marker at the beginning of the round, moving it onto the new first stitch of the round each time you start a new one.

ROUND 10: Now, instead of increasing the number of stitches to make the circle bigger, you'll start decreasing them to make it smaller again and close up the sphere. This is the pattern: (A) single crochet decrease 2 stitches together (see page 156), then (B) single crochet the next 2 stitches the regular way; repeat this until you come to your stitch marker. *You now have* 18 stitches.

ROUND 11: Single crochet decrease 2 stitches together, and then single crochet the next stitch the regular way. Repeat this until you come to your stitch marker. *You now have* 12 stitches.

FILLING

FINISHING

When the opening is fairly small, fill the ball with the popcorn or beans. The smaller the hole, the easier it will be to fill without spilling. Use a funnel if you have one — or make a funnel with a sheet of paper, or use a small spoon (see page 23, step 4).

ROUND 12: Single crochet decrease 2 stitches together. Repeat until you get to the end of the round. *You now have* 6 stitches.

Snip the thread, leaving a 6-inch tail. Pull it all the way through the last stitch and thread the tail onto the blunt sewing needle. Work the tail through the top V of each stitch in the last round; pull the hole closed, then tie off and use the needle to weave in the ends (see page 111), and hide the tails inside the ball.

FIBER CRAFTS FOR EVERYONE!

This is a picture of the gorgeous afghan that Nicole's Pop-pop — er, grandfather — crocheted when he was a young man. Nicole has heard that he made it when he was stationed with the army in North Carolina during basic training. This may or may not be true (you know how families can spin a bit of a *yarn*), but we do love to picture him sitting in the barracks with his crochet hook and a ball of wool while the men around him played poker and did push-ups.

There is, of course, nothing inherently gendered about making things with yarn. Men have always done it, and women have always done it. In the Middle Ages, there were knitting guilds, where men apprenticed to become master knitters, and men knit alongside women during both world wars to make socks and bandages and fingerless gloves for the troops. The Craft Yarn Council estimates that currently two million boys and men are knitters, and Catherine's teenaged son knit a scarf for his best friend (a girl who doesn't knit) for Christmas.

Everybody knits and crochets and sews and weaves and embroiders and felts. Or at least, they should. Because *crafting is awesome*.

WEAVE

If we showed you a big, bulky rag rug with some colors going one way and some the other, you might think, "Weaving." And you'd be right. But weaving is actually everywhere: the denim of your jeans or jacket; the fine, smooth cotton of your button-down shirts or bedsheets; the thick canvas of your tote bag or beach chair. Some fabric, like plaid — with its intersecting stripes of color — makes it easy to see that some threads are

going one way and some are going the other. In other fabric, you can barely make out the distinct threads or yarns, but they're there all the same. Like knitting or crochet, weaving is a way to turn thread or yarn into fabric. (Just think how long it would take you to get dressed every morning if you had to wrap yourself in thread!)

Maybe you've made woven pot holders on a little square loom before (which is really fun!), and you've almost definitely made a friendship bracelet (weaving!) or braided someone's hair (also weaving!), but we're assuming you don't actually have a loom. So while the sky's the limit with, say, knitting and embroidery, where the basic tools are all you need to be as much of an expert as anyone, you can't be a truly masterful weaver without a big, complicated loom. You can still do lots of great smaller weaving projects with just a homemade loom — or with no loom at all. Those are the kinds of projects we're doing in this chapter.

GETTING STARTED

What You Need

Fiber for the warp. These are the threads that will be stretched up and down in your loom before you start weaving. Strong, sturdy cotton or wool thread, string, twine, or yarn is a good choice for the warp threads.

Fiber for the weft. This is the material you will weave back and forth through the warp threads. Like the warp, the weft can be cotton or wool thread, string, twine, or yarn — but it can also be ribbon, shoelaces, strips of fabric, or plants.

Materials to make a loom. Both looms in this chapter are made out of cardboard, from the back of a notepad, say, or from a shoe box or cereal box. You'll also need a pencil, ruler, scissors, and masking tape.

Needles. You'll need a sharp needle for one of the projects and a blunt needle for another.

WHAT? WARP AND WEFT

When it comes to weaving, there are two basic words you need to know, and they both start with a *W: warp* and *weft.* The warp refers to the strings you start with, the up-and-down ones that are pulled super tight before you start. The weft refers to the strings (or other materials) you weave side to side, over and under the warp strings. Here's a trick to remember which one is which: *weft* rhymes with *left* — as in weaving right to left and left to right.

WARP

WEFT

HOW TO
OVER AND UNDER

no cuts here

first "weft" strip

You've probably woven something in your life: a simple construction paper basket, say, or even a complicated friendship bracelet. Just to make sure you have the hang of weaving, though, try this basic "over and under" with two different colors of construction paper. You can make nice greeting cards or bookmarks this way. Just put a little tape on the back of your finished weaving to keep it from coming apart.

1. Cut vertical slits in one piece of paper (the yellow paper above), almost, but not quite, to the end (leave about an inch uncut). This is your warp.

2. Cut the other piece all the way across into strips. This is your weft.

3. Take one weft strip and place it over the first up-and-down warp strip, under the second, over the third, and so on, repeating this over-and-under sequence until you get to the end of your warp strip. If it's not already there, slide the woven weft strip up to the top of the warp.

4. Weave a second weft strip through the warp strips in the same manner, only this time start by going *under* the first warp strip. Slide the completed weft strip up the warp so it's just below the first completed strip.

5. Repeat steps 3 and 4, switching from under-over-under to over-under-over, until you've used all your strips.

DID YOU KNOW? ▶ WEAVING IS *OLD*!

This prehistoric stone loom weight was found in Aylesbeare, England.

Archaeologists in Czechia (also known as the Czech Republic) found a woven textile fossil at the Dolní Věstonice archaeological site that was originally used by mammoth hunters! That means people have been weaving since the Paleolithic era, which didn't even *end* until 10,000 BCE (about 12,000 years ago). An actual piece of cloth woven from hemp plant fibers was found at a different archaeological site in Turkey and dates to 7000 BCE.

WOVEN PATCH

This project is a cross between weaving and embroidery, and it's a favorite of ours — maybe because it's so small and perfect. You can weave a patch to decorate or to repair: add something special to your favorite jacket or cover a hole in your favorite jeans. Try to keep this project small — 1 or 2 inches at most — or it can bunch up the fabric.

WHAT YOU NEED

- Chalk or fabric marker
- Ruler (optional)
- A piece of woven fabric to work on, such as a pair of jeans, denim jacket, or button-down shirt (Knit fabrics like T-shirts are too stretchy to make this project fun.)
- Small embroidery hoop
- Sharp needle
- Perle cotton in two colors (We've done this with embroidery thread, too, but it's more inclined to get split by the needle.)
- Scissors

HOW YOU MAKE IT

SETUP

Use the chalk or fabric marker (and a ruler, if you like) to mark out a square on your fabric. If you're weaving over a hole or tear, leave a wide margin around it so that you're not working where the fabric is weak. Stretch the fabric in your embroidery hoop (see page 50).

MAKING THE WARP

1. Thread your needle (see page 15) with an arm's-length single strand of perle cotton and knot the end (see page 16). At one corner of the square, push the needle up from the back side of the fabric and pull the thread through until the knot is tight against the back of the fabric.

2. Push the needle back down on the opposite side of the square to make a long stitch. This is the first of your warp threads.

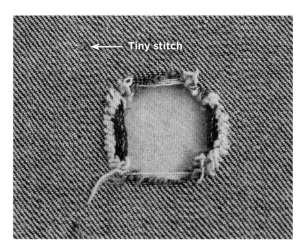

Tiny stitch

3. Push the needle back up through the fabric right next to where you just finished your first warp. This will make a tiny stitch on the back of the fabric.

4. Push the needle back down on the opposite side of the square next to where you started the previous warp thread.

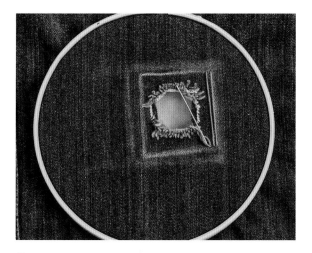

5. Push the needle back up through the fabric immediately next to where you just finished the last warp.

6. Repeat steps 4 and 5 until the whole square is filled with long, close-together warp threads. Tie off the last stitch on the back side of the fabric (see page 17).

MAKING THE WEFT

1. Thread your needle with an arm's length of your second color of perle cotton and knot the end. At a bottom corner of the square, push the needle up from the back side of the fabric, and pull the thread through until the knot is tight against the back of the fabric.

2. Use the needle to weave over and under the warp threads (see page 166), pushing the needle over the first thread and under the second, repeating until you get to the opposite side.

3. Pull the thread all the way through, then make a tiny stitch through the fabric to secure the row you just wove and position your thread for the next weft row. If you ended the previous row by weaving *over* the final warp thread, start this row by weaving *under* the first warp thread.

4. Repeat steps 2 and 3 until your square is filled in, using a fork or your fingers to push the weft threads close together as you go. Tie off the thread on the back of the fabric (see page 17) and snip the end.

DENIM DECONSTRUCTION, BURLAP BREAKDOWN

The next time you have some scrap denim — like from turning your jeans into cutoffs — snip out a square of it. Put it on a cutting board or a piece of paper, then use a needle to pick at the edges. Do you see the weft threads coming away, leaving the warp behind? When your cutoffs fray or fringe, that's what's happening.

Another great fabric to experiment on is burlap, which is that coarsely woven material that flour and grain sacks are sometimes made from. Even before you pick it apart, you can see the weft threads going one way and the warp going another. If you start with a square of burlap, you can actually pull out individual threads and make a pattern. Try it!

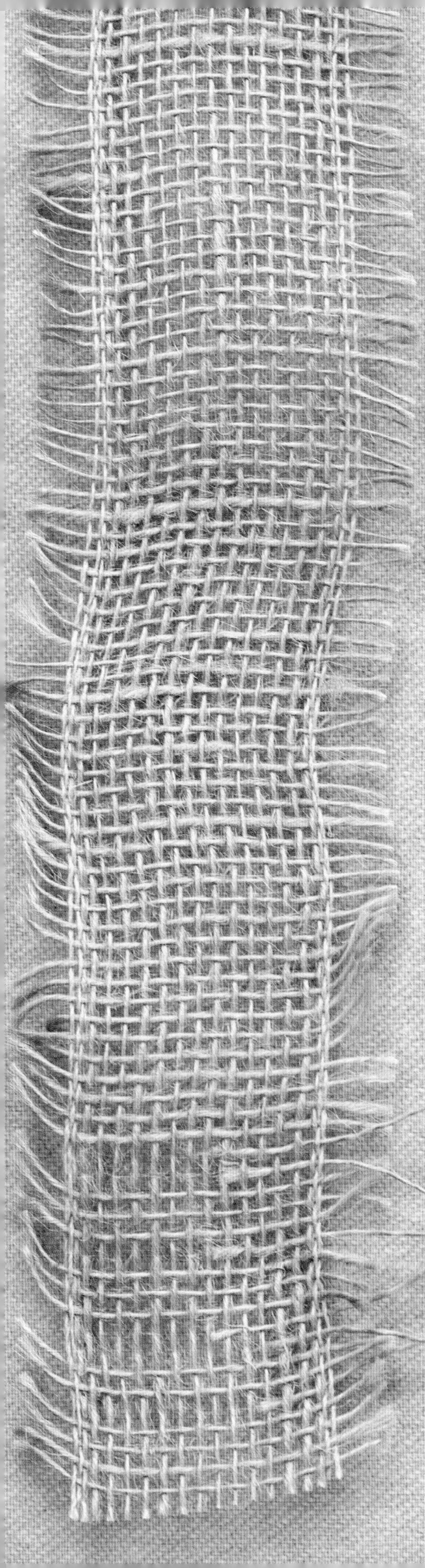

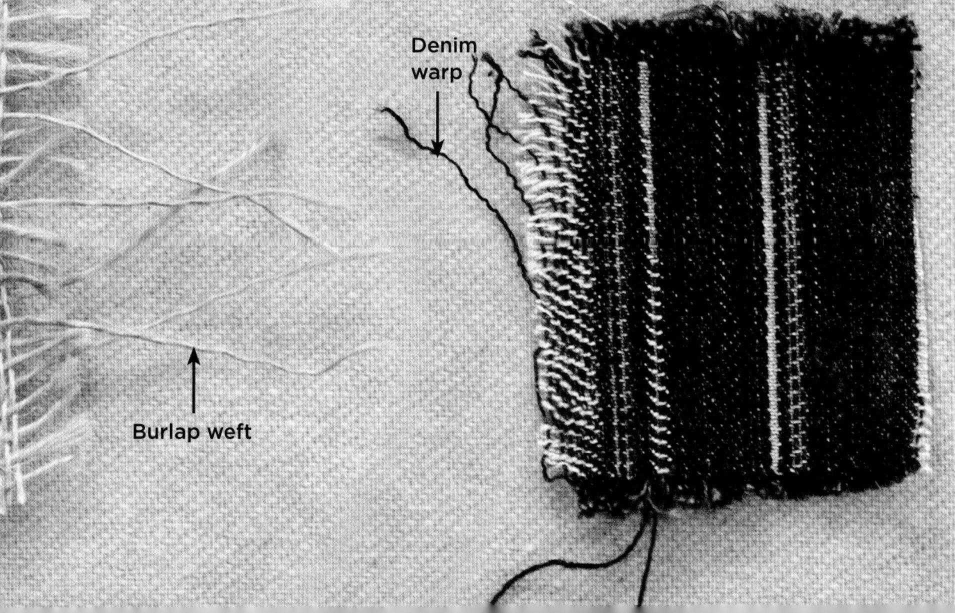

Denim warp

Burlap weft

BEADED KEY FOB
OR NECKLACE

This is a great little project for beginners because you get to make and use a loom. But the loom is nice and small, so you can finish something in one sitting — like this cool key fob, which is just an old-fashioned way of saying *key chain*. The beads give the project enough weight and substance to keep it from getting lost in your pocket — or, if you're making a necklace, from getting tangled in your hair.

WHAT YOU NEED

- 10-inch × 3½-inch piece of heavy cardboard
- Masking tape
- Ruler
- Pencil
- Scissors
- Sturdy string, garden twine, or jute
- Blunt needle with an eye large enough to fit your string
- 6 beads
- Split-ring key ring, carabiner, or swivel-eye lobster snap clasp hook (a long name for a small hook!)

HOW YOU MAKE IT
MAKING AND SETTING UP THE LOOM

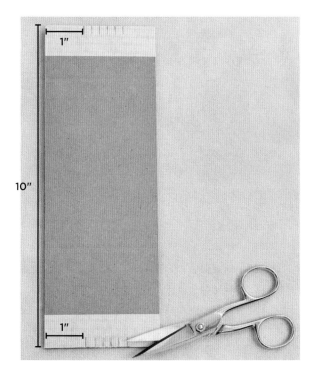

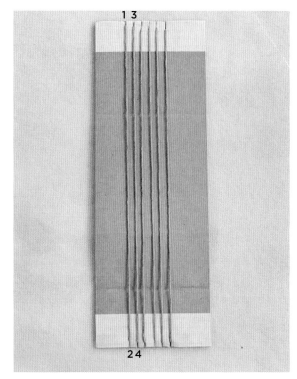

1. Wrap the top and bottom edges of the cardboard with masking tape to make it sturdier. Hold the ruler along the top edge and mark 1 inch in from the edge, and then every ¼ inch until you get to 2¼ inches. *You will have six marks.*

   Repeat along the bottom edge, making six marks at the same intervals. Use your scissors to make a tiny cut — about ¼ inch long — at each mark.

2. To make the warp, tape one end of your string (or twine or jute) to the middle of the back side of the loom. Slot it into the rightmost top slit, then flip the loom over like you're turning a page, so that the front is facing forward (the string will now be on the left).

   Wrap the string down to the bottom side of the cardboard and wedge it into the corresponding notch, then stretch it up the back side, and slot it into the second notch on top, and then down into the matching notch on the bottom. Continue wrapping, pulling the string tight in the notches, moving left to right, until you have six vertical strands.

   Tape the string to the back of the loom, then cut the tail. Run an extra piece of tape across the warp strings on the back to secure them.

WEAVING THE WEFT

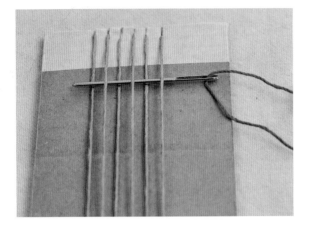

1. Start the weft by cutting about a yard of yarn, string, twine, or jute, and thread your needle (see page 15). Starting about 1 inch from the top of the cardboard, weave the needle under and over the warp threads until you get to the other side (see page 166).

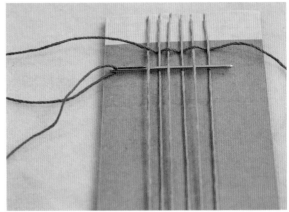

2. Pull the yarn through, leaving a 6-inch tail, then come back the other way, making sure to go *under* the warp threads you went *over* on the previous row, and *over* the warp threads you went *under*.

3. Repeat, going back and forth, until the weaving is as long as you like (this one is about 1 inch), stopping occasionally as you weave to push the rows together snugly with your fingers or the needle. If you want to change colors at any point, simply snip the string you're using, and knot on a different color.

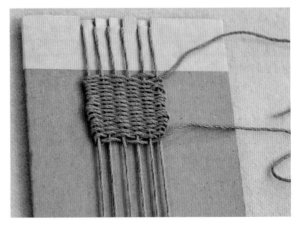

4. At the end of your last row, snip the string, leaving a 6-inch tail.

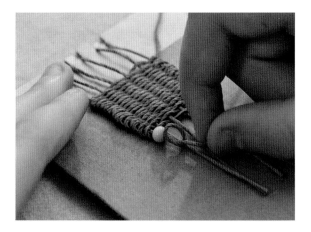

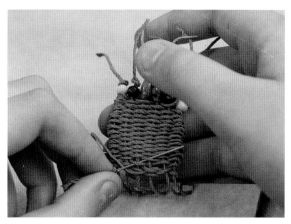

5. Cut across the warp strings 2 inches below your weaving, then thread a bead onto each string and tie a knot below it to secure.

6. Use a needle to weave your two 6-inch weft tails into the back of your weaving, threading each one over and under the weft a few times and then tying them together where they meet in the middle. Snip off the ends.

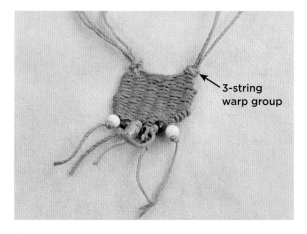

3-string warp group

7. Untape your warp strings and gently remove all the strings from the loom. Separate the warp strings into two groups of three strings each. Knot each set of three warp strings snugly against the weaving.

FOR A KEY FOB

Knot the two sets of warp strings together to make a small loop and snip the ends. Thread the loop onto your key ring.

FOR A NECKLACE

Use a nice soft string or yarn for your weaving so it won't be scratchy on your neck! Follow the directions for Making and Setting Up the Loom and Weaving the Weft through step 7. Knot the two sets of warp strings together at the top to make a long necklace that fits over your head.

If you like to change things up, you can keep the strings loose and tie them each time you wear the necklace, making it a different length, if you want.

TIP◄ FOR BEST RESULTS

...TRY TO KEEP THE WIDTH of your weaving even by not pulling too hard on the weft as you weave.

...PACK THE WEFT IN TIGHTLY (much more tightly than you might even think is possible). You'll want to cover the warp threads completely in order to make a nice, firm fabric. You can use the needle to push each weft thread up against the area you've already woven.

...ADD A PIECE OF TAPE across the front of the warp at the very top before you start weaving. This will help keep the weft from slipping upward when you push your rows tight.

...IF YOU WANT STRIPES, try using variegated yarn (see page 117).

WEAVE EVERYTHING

The more you weave, the more you're going to see weaving potential everywhere. Anything with holes or empty spaces in it, for example, is going to interest you. A colander! A sieve! A tennis racket! A slotted spoon! A forked tree branch! Your Crocs!

But you can also weave over anything that has a flat surface. We decorated this beach rock by winding the warp thread around and around and around, knotting the two ends tightly on the back. We wove the weft with a needle, winding it around the back between rows, and tying the two ends in back when we were done. Paperweight? Art? Weird holiday gift? You decide.

CUT A T-SHIRT INTO A CONTINUOUS STRAND

You can use old T-shirts to make nice thick and colorful weft strips for weaving, or even "yarn" for knitting or crocheting. If you're going to be working with a lot of one color, it's easier to cut the T-shirt a special way so that you can make one continuous strand! Make sure you use a shirt without side seams. And be prepared to clean up lots of tiny nubbles that will come off the shirt as you cut it!

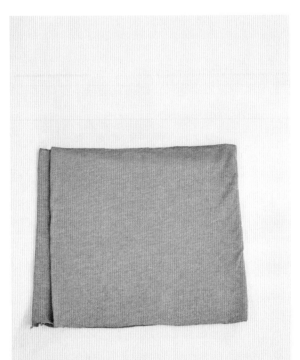

1. Cut a tube of fabric from the middle of the T-shirt, making one horizontal cut just above the bottom hem and one just below the armholes. You'll end up with nice, smooth fabric, without the added seam and bulk of the hem.

2. Fold one side of the tube toward the other side, stopping about 1 inch shy of the edge and smoothing out the fabric.

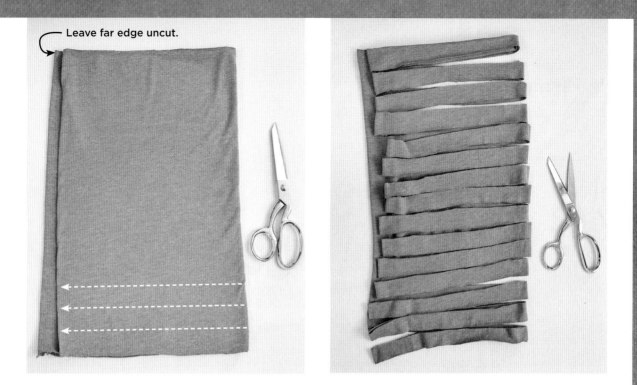

Leave far edge uncut.

3. Going through all four layers of fabric, cut ½- to 1-inch strips from your right-hand fold through the left edge of the top piece.

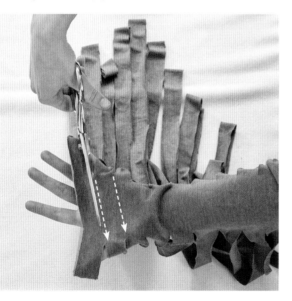

4. Unfold the fabric, slip your arm through the uncut channel, and finish cutting the strips diagonally: from the first strip, cut across to the second strip, and so on until you reach the other end of the fabric.

5. Now you have one continuous strand of fabric. Working in arm-length segments, pull the strand tightly in opposite directions, stretching it to make the strip narrower and curled in, which will allow you to more easily weave or knit with it. Roll it up into a ball, and you're ready to use it!

JAR JACKET

We got the idea for this project from experimenting with using a toilet-paper tube for a loom. A toilet-paper tube makes a super cute — but really small — cylinder of woven fabric. Our loom has an extra step (taping cardboard together to make a tube), but creates something you can really use!

We love this project because it's so much fun to weave around and around. Besides, everyone has old T-shirts kicking around, and this way you can give them new life. And your mason jar drinking glass really needs a new outfit, no? (If it doesn't, this makes a cute wrist cuff for a human.)

WHAT YOU NEED

- Ruler
- Pencil
- 3½-inch × 11-inch piece of cardboard, cut from a cereal box (Use a ruler for measuring, so that the lines will be straight.)
- Scissors
- Clear packing tape
- Sturdy string or twine
- Old T-shirts
- Large-eyed blunt needle

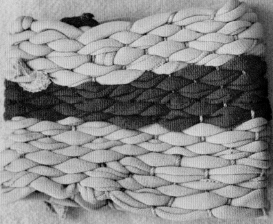

HOW YOU MAKE IT
MAKING AND SETTING UP THE LOOM

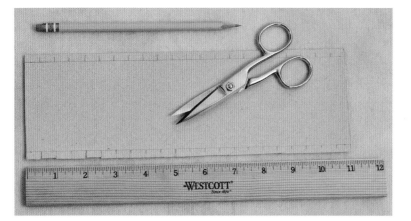

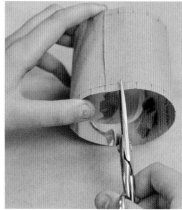

1. Use the ruler to draw a straight line across the top and bottom of the cardboard, about ¼ inch in from the edge. These will be your cutting guides. Mark every ½ inch along the top edge and make sure you have an odd number of marks! Repeat along the bottom edge.

    Cut along each mark, making sure to go only as far as the cutting guide. These will be the slots for your warp thread.

2. Curve the cardboard into a tube, overlapping the edges exactly ½ inch, then secure well with tape. The tape will probably cover one of the slits, and you should recut that one.

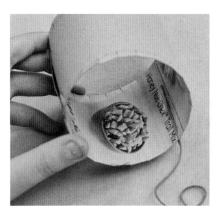

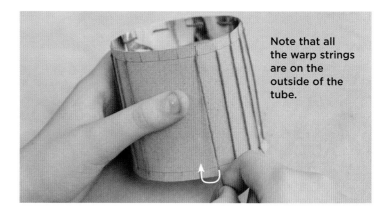

Note that all the warp strings are on the outside of the tube.

3. To start setting up the warp, slide the string or twine into the notch nearest the tape, leaving a 2-inch tail inside the tube. Tape the tail down to secure it.

4. Pull the string down to the corresponding notch at the bottom of the tube, and slide it in, pulling the string taut. Now tug the string over into the next notch (you'll make a little dash of string inside the tube), and stretch it up across the tube into the corresponding notch above. Then pull the string one notch over and down. Repeat this until you have strung the warp up and down around the entire tube.

    When you get back to where you started, leave a 2-inch tail and snip the thread, then tape the tail inside the tube.

WEAVING THE JAR JACKET

1. Cut long ½-inch-wide strips of fabric from your T-shirts. (It's fine if they're a little raggedy and imperfect!) Or learn how to cut your shirt into one continuous strand (see page 178).

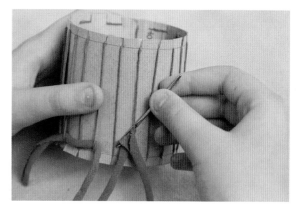

2. Thread your needle with one T-shirt strip and begin weaving near the tape at the bottom of the tube, leaving a 2-inch tail. Weave the fabric over and under (see page 166) the warp strings, around and around the tube, pulling it through as you go.

3. When you have about 3 inches of weft fabric left, stop, remove the needle, knot a new piece (or a new color) to the old one, and snip the ends. Rethread your needle and keep weaving, carefully pulling the knot through so that the weft stays nice and tight. (Don't worry: the knots will end up on the back!)

4. Keep weaving, stopping occasionally to push the weft together so that it stays snug, until you get to the very top of the tube. (You want to cram in as much as you can, so the weaving will be nice and tight and all of the warp strings will be covered by the T-shirt weft strings.) Finish your weft row at the tape.

5. Cut your weft strip, leaving a 3-inch tail, then untape the warp from the inside of the tube. Tie the weft and warp strands together. Repeat at the bottom, knotting the original weft tail to the warp tail.

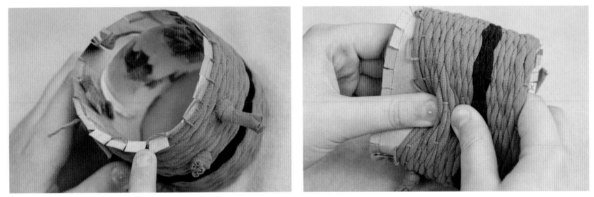

6. Fold the cardboard tabs at the top toward you to release the warp loops from the back. Repeat with the tabs at the bottom of the tube, then fold the cardboard slightly to let the weaving slide off.

7. Turn your weaving inside out so the knots are on the inside.

FOR FUN

DIY LOOMS

If you've got the weaving bug now, you can make a bigger loom out of any number of different materials: a cardboard box, a picture frame, a chair that has no bottom, or PVC pipe, which you can get at the hardware store.

Kids Weaving, by Sarah Swett, has complete directions for making a PVC pipe loom, and there are also lots of websites with directions for all kinds of DIY (do-it-yourself) looms. (In the picture above, Catherine's daughter is at the Snow Farm craft center weaving a T-shirt rug on a giant

pot holder–style loom that our friend Crispina ffrench made from wood and screws!) Of course, you can also make *smaller* looms. A matchbox makes a fun loom frame for the tiniest projects.

GLOSSARY

B

BULKY-WEIGHT YARN. A thick yarn, which we use a lot because it's warm and it knits up quickly. You might also see it called *chunky* yarn.

C

CARBON TRANSFER PAPER. Paper that's been treated on one side with a black (or white or different color) coating. It's also sold as *dressmaker's carbon* or *graphite transfer paper*. You use it to transfer a design to your fabric for embroidering.

CIRCULAR KNITTING NEEDLES. Knitting needles connected by a line of flexible plastic (or wire), so instead of switching hands to knit back and forth and make a rectangle, you can just keep knitting around and around to make a tube.

D

DK-WEIGHT YARN. A lightweight yarn that's thinner than *worsted weight* and much thinner than *bulky weight*. DK stands for "double knitting," which refers to the weight of the yarn, not a technique you might use it in.

DOUBLE-POINTED NEEDLES. Knitting needles with points at both ends that come in sets of four or five. You use them to knit circular projects (such as hats, socks, or I-cords) in the round.

E

EMBROIDERY FLOSS. A 6-strand thread used for sewing and embroidery. It comes in tons of colors and can be shiny and metallic or cottony and plain. You can use all 6 strands at once, or you can pull a piece apart into two 3-strand lengths or three 2-strand lengths.

F

FABRIC. Any textile (also called *cloth*) that you make from weaving, knitting, crocheting, or felting individual strands of fiber.

FELT. As a noun, *felt* refers to matted fibers turned into a smooth fabric that doesn't fray at the edges when you cut it. As a verb, *felt* means washing and drying fabric so that the fibers shrink and mat together into a kind of material that doesn't fray when you cut it.

FLEECE. As a material, this is a thick, soft synthetic fabric — also known as *polar fleece* — that doesn't fray when you cut it. When talking about animals, *fleece* is a sheep's woolly covering!

FRAY. To come apart at a cut edge. Fraying can be prevented by hemming the fabric or using either felt or polar fleece, which don't fray.

H

HEM. To fold under the edge of a piece of fabric or a garment and sew it down so that it doesn't fray or look raggedy. As a noun, *hem* means the sewn edge of fabric.

N

NEEDLE THREADER. A small device for helping to put thread through the eye of a needle. It's usually a thin, pointed loop of wire attached to a little metal disc.

P

PATTERN. In sewing, a paper version of the fabric pieces you'll need to stitch together to make your garments. Typically, you trace around the paper pattern onto the fabric.

R

RIBBING. The ridged, stretchy cuff or bottom edge of a sweater or T-shirt.

RIGHT SIDE. The side you hope shows when your project is done: it's the side of the fabric where you can see the printed pattern or where your embroidery is clear (versus the side that has all the knots) or the side of your knitting that looks best to you. When you're knitting on circular needles, the *right side* usually refers to the side that looks like vertical columns of *V*s.

ROW. In knitting or crochet, a complete line of stitches. At the end of a knit row, you switch the needles hand to hand. At the end of a crochet row, you make a turning chain.

S

SEAM. The line of stitches where two pieces — or two edges of the same piece — of fabric are joined together.

T

TAIL. The cut end of yarn or thread in knitting, crochet, sewing, or weaving, either at the start of your project, at the end of it, or when you switch colors.

TAUT. Pulled tight. In sewing or embroidery, this refers to the fabric; in knitting or crochet, this refers to the yarn.

TURNING CHAIN. In crochet, this is the extra stitch you make between finishing one row and starting the next. It makes room in your piece for it to grow evenly.

U

UNRAVEL. The process of the fibers coming apart, usually when you don't want them to. This can refer to yarn or to something you've knit or crocheted with yarn.

W

WOOL. The fleece of an animal — especially a sheep — or the yarn spun from it.

WORKING YARN. The yarn coming freshly off the ball that you're using as you knit or crochet.

WORSTED-WEIGHT YARN. Yarn of average thickness; what you probably picture when you picture yarn. It's good for most knitting projects but knits up a little less quickly than *bulky* yarn.

Y

YARN. A long, continuous length of spun fibers — either natural or synthetic — used for knitting, crocheting, and weaving.

YARNOVER. In crochet, the action of wrapping the working yarn over the hook from the back to the front.

ADDITIONAL READING

These are some books that we've found useful, organized according to craft.

SEW

Alabama Stitch Book: Projects and Stories Celebrating Hand-Sewing, Quilting, and Embroidery for Contemporary Sustainable Style, Natalie Chanin and Stacie Stukin (Stewart, Tabori and Chang, 2008).

Generation T: 108 Ways to Transform a T-Shirt, Megan Nicolay (Workman, 2006).

Improv Sewing: A Freeform Approach to Creative Techniques, Nicole Blum and Debra Immergut (Storey, 2012).

Mend It Better: Creative Patching, Darning, and Stitching, Kristin M. Roach (Storey, 2012).

One-Yard Wonders, Patricia Hoskins and Rebecca Yaker (Storey, 2009).

Simple Sewing: Patterns and How-To for 24 Fresh and Easy Projects, Lotta Jansdotter (Chronicle Books, 2007).

EMBROIDER

All About Embroidery, Todd Oldham (Ammo Books, 2012).

The Amazing Stitching Handbook for Kids: 17 Embroidery Stitches, 15 Fun & Easy Projects, Kristin Nicholas (C&T Publishing, 2015).

Cool Embroidery for Kids: A Fun and Creative Introduction to Fiber Art, Alex Kuskowski (Checkerboard Books, 2014).

FELT

Felt Fantastic: Over 25 Brilliant Things to Make with Felt, Sarah Tremelling (David & Charles, 2013).

Knit One, Felt Too: Discover the Magic of Knitted Felt with 25 Easy Patterns, Kathleen Taylor (Storey, 2003).

The Sweater Chop Shop: Sewing One-of-a-Kind Creations from Recycled Sweaters, Crispina ffrench (Storey, 2009).

Sweater Surgery: How to Make New Things with Old Sweaters, Stefanie Girard (Quarry, 2008).

KNIT

Finger Knitting Fun: 28 Cute, Clever, and Creative Projects for Kids, Vickie Howell (Quarry, 2015).

How to Knit: Learn the Basic Stitches and Techniques, Leslie Ann Bestor (Storey, 2014).

Kids Knit! Simple Steps to Nifty Projects, Sarah Bradberry (Sterling, 2006).

Kids Knitting: Projects for Kids of All Ages, Melanie Falick (Artisan, 2003).

Last-Minute Knitted Gifts, Joelle Hoverson (Stewart, Tabori and Chang, 2004).

Mason-Dixon Knitting: The Curious Knitters´ Guide: Stories, Patterns, Advice, Opinions, Questions, Answers, Jokes, and Pictures, Kay Gardiner and Ann Meador Shayne (Potter Craft, 2006).

Susan B. Anderson's Kids' Knitting Workshop: The Easiest and Most Effective Way to Learn to Knit, Susan B. Anderson (Artisan, 2015).

CROCHET

Crochet for Kids: Basic Techniques & Great Projects that Kids Can Make Themselves, Franziska Heidenreich (Stackpole Books, 2014).

How to Crochet: Learn the Basic Stitches and Techniques, Sara Delaney (Storey, 2014).

Kids Crochet: Projects for Kids of All Ages, Kelli Ronci (Stewart, Tabori & Chang, 2005).

WEAVE

Friendship Bracelets 101: Fun to Make, Fun to Wear, Fun to Share, Suzanne McNeill (Fox Chapel Publishing, 2001).

Inventive Weaving on a Little Loom: Discover the Full Potential of the Rigid-Heddle Loom, for Beginners and Beyond, Syne Mitchell (Storey, 2015).

Kids Weaving: Projects for Kids of All Ages, Sarah Swett (Stewart, Tabori & Chang, 2005).

THANK YOU, THANK YOU, THANK YOU
(AKA ACKNOWLEDGMENTS)

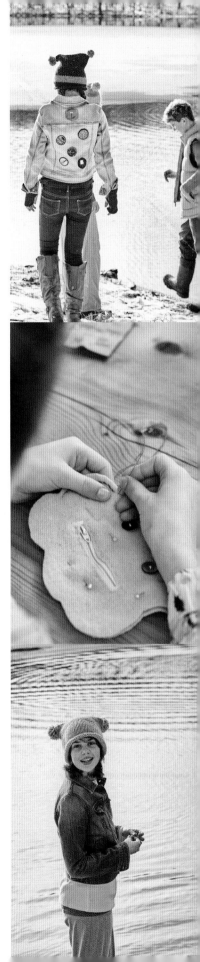

This book, like all books, has the hands and minds of so many brilliant, generous, and loving people on every page.

Our team at Storey is made up of the most dedicated, talented, and creative people: Gwen Steege originally proposed the book to us and buoyantly shepherded it through its early phases. Michal Lumsden graciously took it on and dedicated her enthusiasm (and countless hours of work) to perfecting the projects. We prayed that Carolyn Eckert would design the book — and she did! Every beautiful page has her brilliance all over it. Margaret Lampert took the gorgeous photos that brought the projects to life, and her assistant, David Kurtis, was a model of good humor and expertise. Our meticulous technical editors and crafters — Dianne de Mott, Heather McQueen, and Jessica Miller-Smith — made sure that the projects worked, worked well, and were pretty to boot. We are lucky to have Alee Moncy and Sarah Armour cheering this book on and spreading the good word. And Deborah Balmuth, our publisher, is simply the greatest visionary and champion that anyone could hope for.

Sara Delaney patiently and selflessly taught us how to crochet — and any mistakes we continue to make are not her fault! We are also grateful to WEBS, the yarn store where she worked, for donating so much gorgeous yarn to our projects (special shout-out to their Berkshire line of yarn, which we love knitting with). We'd also like to thank all our friends and family, for friendship and kinship, and you our readers, for your willingness to fill your hands with crafting.

We were so lucky to have these beautiful, patient, and hardworking crafters and models: Ava Blum-Carr, Harry Blum-Carr, Inez Dole, Layla Elkalai, Sahar Elkalai, Roy Gentes, Katherine Kang, Finn Mead, Claire Michaels, Ben Newman, Birdy Newman, Jamie Park, April Schilling, Jenna Schilling, Zoe te Velde, plus our patient working models: Annabel Charles, Madison Davies, Adam Etwaroo, Ishan Jain, and Kaitlyn Vittum.

We are lucky in love: Jonathan and Michael were very patient and helpful while we sat around, knitting and drinking tea, and called it "work." Thank you for that, and everything else.

METRIC CONVERSION CHART

TO CONVERT	TO	MULTIPLY
inches	millimeters	inches by 25.4
inches	centimeters	inches by 2.54
inches	meters	inches by 0.0254
feet	meters	feet by 0.3048
yards	meters	yards by 0.9144

STANDARD EQUIVALENTS

US	METRIC
⅛ inch	3.2 mm
¼ inch	6.35 mm
⅜ inch	9.5 mm
½ inch	1.27 cm
⅝ inch	1.59 cm
¾ inch	1.91 cm
⅞ inch	2.22 cm
1 inch	2.54 cm

INDEX

STITCH TOGETHER
YOUR CREATIVITY LIBRARY
WITH MORE BOOKS FROM STOREY

by Amie Petronis Plumley & Andria Lisle
Kids can complete these 21 inspired hand-sewing projects with minimal supervision. Step-by-step photographed instructions teach basic sewing skills, then put them to use making pillows, dolls, blankets, totes, and more.

by Amie Petronis Plumley & Andria Lisle
For kids ages 7 and up who have mastered hand sewing, this book's photographs and step-by-step instructions for machine-sewing 20 creative projects will open up a world of exciting possibilities!

by Nicole Blum & Debra Immergut
You'll love sewing these playful one-of-a-kind accessories and imaginative home decor items. Easy instructions mean you can create any of the 101 beautiful and freestyle projects in less than a day.

by Crispina ffrench
Repurpose wool sweaters to create cool clothes, one-of-a-kind toys, and handy household items. Diagrams and detailed directions guide you through making zippered cardigans, rag dolls, potholders, and so much more!

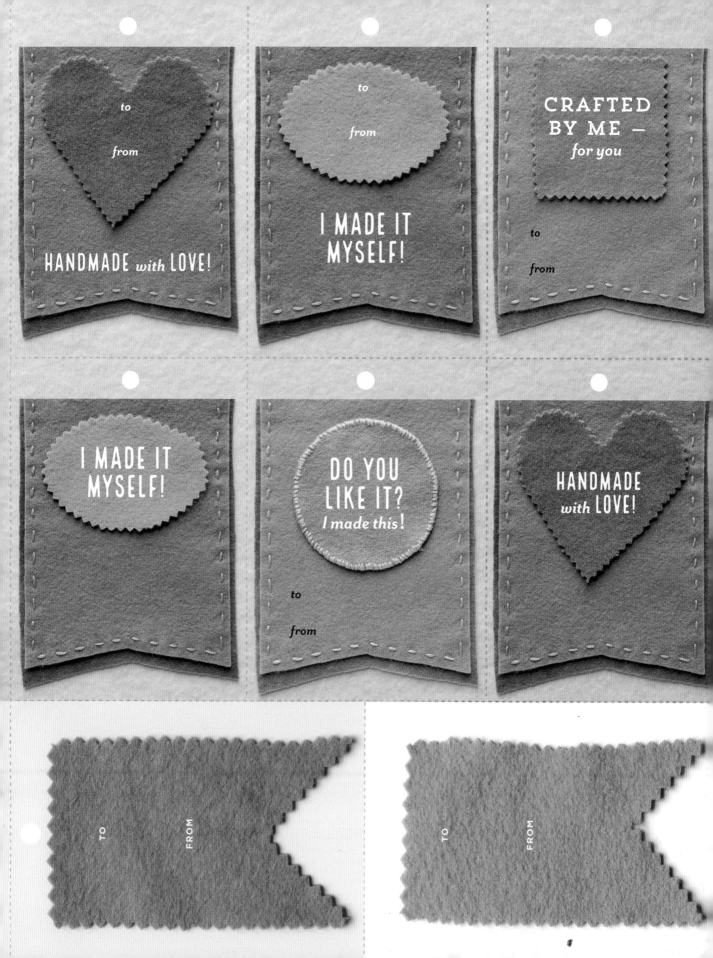

HANDMADE
with LOVE!

to

from

HANDMADE
with LOVE!

to

from

to

from

HANDMADE
with LOVE!

to

from

TO

FROM

to

from

to

from

to

from

HANDMADE
with LOVE!

to

from

to

from

to

from